CHILD OF THE WORLD

Montessori, Global Education
for Age 3-12+

Susan Mayclin Stephenson

CHILD OF THE WORLD
Montessori, Global Education for Age 3-12+
Copyright © 2013 by Susan Mayclin Stephenson

Michael Olaf Montessori Company
PO Box 1162
Arcata, CA 95518, USA
www.michaelolaf.net
michaelola@aol.com

Parts of this book were previously published in *Child of the World, Essential Montessori for 3-12+*, 2001-2010 editions

ISBN 1-879264-24-2
ISBN 978-1-879264-24-3

Cover: A rendition of an oil painting by the author, her gift of Russian matreshka dolls, given to a Tibetan child, in India

Illustrations: except for the photo on page154 all of the main photos were taken by the author who would like to express her gratitude to the families, and school personnel for this privilege.

Printed in the United States of America

I live in heaven.

My home is a sphere that travels around the sun.

It is called Earth.

—Maria Montessori, MD

CONTENTS

INTRODUCTION

Global education has two meanings. The most common refers to the excellent efforts, particularly of non-profits, to bring literacy and better health practices to parts of the globe where it is most needed.

But there is another, deeper, more powerful meaning: to give every child "a vision of the universe and his place in it." These are Maria Montessori's words. They are not a utopian fantasy, but rather a *goal* that Montessori has set for humanity. It was her wish that human beings might reflect on their condition and set about consciously to create a wiser, more compassionate, more peaceful world.

What if every child, everywhere, could grow up trusting in the world, and trusting in himself, herself, to have the power to collaborate with other cultures, to contribute to the earth in unique and peaceful ways?

Susan Stephenson, with excellent training and many years of experience with children of all ages around the world, writes with genuine wisdom, compassion and a voice filled with enthusiasm. She shows us many of the possibilities. Be inspired.

—**Karin Salzmann**, founding director of the Association Montessori Internationale in the United States

PART ONE, AGE 3-6

CARING FOR ONESELF, FOR OTHERS, AND FOR THE ENVIRONMENT

Boys at a Montessori school in Bhutan preferring to work on fixing the school sidewalk than to play.

When I was young I agreed with my friends, none of us having any experience parenting and teaching so far, that children were more interesting to spend time with when they were older and more able to learn. Boy was I wrong! Now I realize that more learning goes on in the first six years of life than ever again. During the first six years of life a child absorbs, like a sponge, the world around him. Without effort he takes in the language, culture, attitudes, manners, values, and interactions of those around him, and this all becomes a part of him forever. By age six he becomes fully a member of a particular culture and family group. A child who spends these first years in a loving and supportive environment learns to feel safe in the world, and when he is allowed to develop as a fully functioning and contributing member of his group he learns to feel valuable, needed, and to like himself.

One of the great discoveries in the Montessori world in the past 100-plus years is that children are not empty slates with a need to be filled up, or rewarded into working, learning, concentrating, being kind. These are natural tendencies of the human being and should be protected. Every child, by instinct, wants to learn and grow to the limit of his abilities. To support this need we must carefully prepare the physical and social environment, provide tools that enable the child to work to create himself, watch for those first tentative moments of concentration, and get out of the way, following the child as his path unfolds. We call the activities through which he creates himself "work" rather than "play" only because the use of this word reminds us adults to respect and not to interrupt the child. This work not only fulfills the child's potential but also seems to be the most powerful force in creating the peace in the world we all long for.

When the children had completed an absorbing bit of work, they appeared rested and deeply pleased. It almost seemed as if a road had opened up within their souls that led to all their latent powers, revealing the better part of themselves. They exhibited a great affability to everyone, put themselves out to help others, and seemed full of good will.

— Maria Montessori

Today the importance of the formative first six years in predicting success in life is common knowledge in many fields. In her keynote speech at the Annual General Meeting of The Association Montessori International (AMI) Adele Diamond, one of the world's leading neuroscientists, argued that *in order to create, one must be in the moment and be allowed to stay there.*

Respecting, not interrupting, a child's concentration is central to Montessori philosophy.

Adele has observed the value of learning by doing, and by being allowed to repeat; the value of being allowed to endlessly repeat an activity, such as doing a puzzle, has been understood in Montessori classes for more than a century. The adult clearly and slowly demonstrates the activity to the child once, but there is no way to predict if the child will carry out an activity one time or thirty times; it is left to the child to decide when to stop. Dr. Diamond tells us that programs, such as Montessori, that address the whole child, cognitive, emotional, social, spiritual, and physical, seem to be most successful at improving any one of these areas.

Perhaps most importantly, she tells us that in order to really understand that practicing compassion makes the doer happy, children need to experience the joy that

5

comes from putting a smile on someone else's face, not just hear about it, and it must be repeated and practiced daily. This is observed at all levels of Montessori where it is considered a natural human tendency, and part of the curriculum, to teach, help, and care for peers.

The child can only develop by means of experience in his environment. We call such experience work.

—Maria Montessori

During a summer visit these two enjoyed spending more than an hour cleaning grandmother's kitchen!

The traditional work of the family is referred to in Montessori as practical life work. It is the single most important area of an education for life. The activities of practical life are generally thought of in three main categories, and looking at the child's life in this way helps to keep a balance in the activities we offer children in the home or at school. These areas of practical life depend on the culture in which the child is growing up, and may include, but are not limited to:

1) *Care of the environment*—cleaning, sweeping, polishing, hanging up clothing, washing clothes, gardening, putting away toys, cooking, setting the table.

2) *Care of the person*—bathing, dressing, brushing teeth, combing hair, cleaning shoes.

3) *Grace and courtesy*—walking carefully, carrying things, opening and closing a door, tucking in a chair when finishing work, rolling up a floor mat, offering food, table manners, saying "please" and "thank you" and so on.

It is in learning to do such seemingly mundane activities as dressing, dusting, sweeping, preparing and serving food, and fixing or building-work that a child sees going on around him all day long-that he learns to use his body and mind for a *purpose*, to plan, to concentrate, to control his actions, to finish what he started. These abilities are the *Executive Functions* (EFs) that Adele Diamond is researching, and that are considered more important than IQ in predicting success in university and in life. Most importantly, with this work, the child is able to see himself contributing to the important work of the family, the social group.

Practical life activities provide superior groundwork for physical, mental, and social development, and teach the work habits that lead to success in all later academic work and in all aspects of later life. Practical life work provides practice in eye-hand coordination, the control of large and small muscles, and the ability to walk and to carry objects with control, and to behave with knowledge of good manners. These are the activities that bring the child's attention to his own progress and development, and that open up a world of important work. Learning to look a person in the eye when speaking, to listen patiently, to exhibit thoughtfulness through good manners, enables the child to be welcomed into a social group, to be happy and to make others happy.

Children have for eons shown an interest in daily life through make-believe cooking and cleaning. It was one of the pivotal discoveries of Dr. Montessori that, given the chance, children usually choose real work over imaginary. Allowing the child to participate in the daily work he sees going on around him is an act of great respect for, and confidence in, the child. It helps him to feel important to himself and to those around him. He is needed. We can empathize if we think about the difference in our own treatment of a dinner guest in our home that we serve and wait upon, compared to the different treatment of a good friend who is welcomed in our kitchen to talk and laugh while we prepare the meal together. Children don't want to be the guest; they want us to help them to do it themselves.

The child's purpose, his approach to working is different from ours. Adults will usually choose to do things the most efficient and quickest way and to rush through or avoid anything labeled "work." A child, on the other hand, is working to master the activity and to practice and perfect his abilities. He may scrub a table each day for weeks, then turn his attention to some other activity to master and stop scrubbing tables because he is busy with new challenges. We must not look upon this method as inconsistency or laziness but rather cumulative mastery of abilities.

Sometimes the parent is confused, thinking because a child learned to clear the table after a meal, or help sort the laundry, and then stops doing these activities, that something has gone wrong, that the parent should remind the child to continue to do these things. But think again. There would not be time in the day if the child continued to do every single thing he learned, every single day! The child's purpose at this age is not to complete the task as much as to construct the self. It is later, when the child is in the next developmental stage between ages 6-12 that he will work out of responsibility to his group.

Real, child size materials support a child's important work, at home and at school.

Practical life or real work activities, along with the development of language, may well be the most important work in the first six years of life. By means of these activities the child learns to make intelligent choices, to become physically and mentally independent and responsible. He learns to concentrate, to control muscles, to act with care, to focus, to analyze logical steps, and complete a cycle of activity. This lays the groundwork for sound mental and physical work throughout life.

THE PREPARATION AND SERVING OF FOOD

In a classroom in Moscow, potatoes, cabbage, and beets are prepared for making soup.

Arranging the cooking and dining areas for the work of the child does not have to be a giant undertaking, and it does not need to be done all at once. Consider giving the child one low shelf or one drawer in the kitchen in the beginning. This could contain a cutting board and safe knife, or cereal bowls and spoons — whatever the child is most likely to use most often. A stool is a good first investment, so the child can reach the sink or the counter, for work. Even better, if there is room, have a small table and chair or stool out of the way where the child can prepare and eat snacks, or do his share of the food preparation. In the classroom, there can be a space for children to prepare food at any time of the day, and lessons on how to do this work and on how to clean it up, in preparation for use by the next child.

This is an exercise in contributing to the good of others—preparing and serving food, and cleaning up so it is ready for a friend.

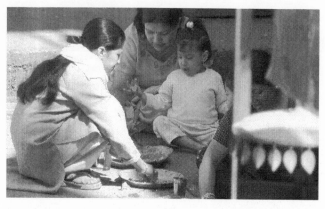

A child wants to learn the good manners of his or her own culture; in Nepal this means how to eat properly with one's fingers.

Practical tasks help lay the foundation for all later mental and physical work. It is not uncommon for the value of *practical life* to be misunderstood. I have heard parents exclaim in dismay that their child is, "wasting time cleaning in her new Montessori school when she should be doing math!" However, math and all other intellectual work requires the ability to move carefully, to focus, to complete sequential steps, to concentrate, to make intelligent choices and to persevere in one's work. This is exactly what is learned during this kind of work. As a result of periods of time spent concentrating on such a task a child becomes focused, calm, patient, and satisfied, and the foundation for math and other academic work will be made firm.

Perhaps an even more important result of the work connected with the preparation and serving of food is that the child sees himself already as an important and contributing member of the group, a respected and intimate friend, when he is welcome to participate in the work of the adult. The child benefits in many ways from this close working relationship with the parent, whether it be in scrubbing or cutting up the vegetables, washing or drying the dishes, setting the table, cleaning out the cupboards or refrigerator, mixing the muffin batter, and so forth. When a child has a lot of experience with the important developmental tasks called practical life he becomes more successful in all other areas of study and in relating to others.

The most important discovery is that a child returns to a normal state through work. Countless experiments made upon children of every race throughout the world have shown that this is the most certain datum that we have in the field of psychology and education. A child's desire to work represents a vital instinct since he cannot organize his personality without working: a man builds himself through working. There can be no substitute for work; neither affection nor physical well being can replace it. A man builds himself by carrying out manual labor in which he uses his hands as the instruments of his personality and as an expression of his intellect and will help him to dominate his environment. A child's instinct for work is a proof that work is instinctive to man and characteristic of the species.

...if we showed them exactly how to do something, this precision itself seemed to hold their interest. To have a real purpose to which the action was directed, this was the first condition, but the exact way of doing it acted like a support which rendered the child stable in his efforts, and therefore brought him to make progress in his development. Order and precision, we found, were the keys to spontaneous work in the school.

— **Maria Montessori**

Parents do not always have the time in today's fast-paced world to include the child in everything and should not feel bad about this. It is different in the Montessori classroom when the teacher is available to the child for this work all day long, and trained to give lessons and help the child grow toward independence. She is not trying to balance this work with all of endeavors of a parent. It is too much to expect a new parent, or a busy parent to do this perfectly. We must be easy on ourselves in the home and plan a time when we will enjoy work as well as the children. Begin with just one thing, perhaps putting the napkins on the table for a meal, and gradually add to the tasks in which the child can participate, and eventually take over.

Compost bucket, a place to prepare and have a meal, even a coffee grinder for preparing guests' coffee, all are found in a Montessori classroom.

In the end this effort on the part of the parent pays off for the adult as well as the child as we observe that the child's method of working is not just to get the task finished, but also to enjoy it! This can actually help the parent take time off from thinking about the past and the future and just be mindful of the present moment. One of the most important lessons we can learn from the child is how to bring our whole selves, mentally, physically, and spiritually, to the task at hand, to focus on each thing we do, and to enjoy each moment of life. This is a gift from the child if we can take the time to accept it.

I remember once reading a study on the happiness and success of teenagers. A group of the happiest, balanced, most successful, and healthiest teenagers were identified by their peers and teachers and studied to find out what they had in common in their upbringing, experience, environment, etc. if anything. There was no correlation with family social status, economic level, race, religion, types of school, private classes, camps, I.Q., or anything else as obvious. The only thing that they had in common was that they shared a meal once a day with the rest of their family, without the radio or the television turned on. It did not matter which meal, how long the family sat together, or any of the other details of a meal. The implications of the value of spending time each day communicating with a group of people who care about each other, give us a lot to think about. Life has changed, but the need to feel a part of a group has not. Cooking and eating are something everyone does every day. Perhaps taking a few moments to work together to cook something, to set the table, just one little thing each day, can keep the whole family on the path to wholeness.

TOYS AND GAMES

Blocks, homemade or bought, and a place to keep them, are among the most creative toys ever.

We have to understand that the world can only be grasped by action, not by contemplation. The hand is more important than the eye. It is the hand that drives the subsequent evolution of the brain. I have described the hand when it uses a tool as an instrument of discovery. We see that every time a child learns — to lace his shoes, to thread a needle, to fly a kite or to play a penny whistle.

With the practical action there goes another, namely finding pleasure in action for its own sake — in the skill that one perfects by being pleased with it. This at the bottom is responsible for every work of art, and science too: our poetic delight in what

human beings do because they can do it. The hand is
the cutting edge of the mind.
— Jacob Bronowski (mathematician, biologist,
science historian), *The Ascent of Man*

It takes work on the part of the adult to withstand the temptation to let the child spend hours in front of the television, the computer, or other screens, but it is well worth the effort to support the natural development of the child. Television accustoms the child to be a passive receiver of information rather than an active questioner or researcher. And the intelligence of computers does not hold a candle to the kind of creativity inborn in the human being. The child at this age needs a lot of movement, outside in nature if possible, to be healthy. He needs large muscle movement and gradually more and more refined large and small muscles — legs, trunk, arms, hands, to the pincer movement of thumb and fingers.

The young child is vividly aware of the world, taking in impressions through all of her senses. This is the time of life when habits are formed, to help lay the groundwork for the child's ability to think, experience, and create throughout life. We take special care in providing toys that support this development, toys made of natural materials. Toys rich in variety of weight, color, texture, and purpose, of the best quality available, engage the child's intelligence as well as his body. The child needs opportunities to explore and classify sensorial impressions, different smells, tastes, and sounds. For example at first maybe just offer the experience of the primary colors of red, blue and yellow, but then the secondary colors, and then shades of all colors. Then we can give sensorial games such as looking for all of the red objects in the environment. Or the experience of smelling herbs, and then a game of guessing which herb is being held in front of his nose with his eyes closed or covered.

At first the child will become aware of the difference between a large cube and a small one, but then much more variation in size and practice putting objects in order by size, or looking for the *thick* book, then a *thicker* book, then the *thickest* book of all. Remember it is during the first six years that the child can easily take in and store all of this information that will be used throughout life in all creative work.

There are special toys or what might be thought of as sensorial *puzzles* in the Montessori school to isolate and teach specific concepts through repeated individual work of the child. A few examples you may have heard of include the pink tower, the color tablets, and the sound boxes. They clearly illustrate concepts such as large and small, light and dark, loud and soft and so on. These materials have a specific way to be used because it is in this way that the child develops an understanding of the concept each is designed to teach. They are considered keys to open the door, each to teach one concept.

Sometimes people misunderstand the importance of sticking to the intended use of these materials and wonder why children cannot use them in any way they please. I sometimes explain that they can be thought of as puzzles or puzzle toys because there is a specific solution that is sought, a specific way to use them or to put them together, the yellow color tablets matching, the large cube of the pink tower at the bottom and the smallest at the top of the tower. The uses of these materials are as specific as the use of woodworking, cooking tools, or musical instruments. One does not for example use a violin to pound a nail, or a hammer to play a drum.

These sensorial materials have no place in the home. But the parent can keep the lessons, the concepts, in mind and play with the child in the way suggested above in order to help a child classify his sensorial impressions. The understanding of such concepts contributes to the creativity of the child in the home — feeling the temperature of the bath water, exploring tastes while baking, and color or size with flowers, textures of fabrics, etc.

Different than puzzle toys with specific uses are those with open-ended uses. These also teach valuable skills. For example a child learns how to hold a nail and use a hammer safely, and after learning the correct use of a hammer, he can create pictures of any design with the hammer board. The use of the hammer and nails is specific, but the patterns made are as open-ended. Playing with blocks and animal models in the home can provide hours of creative exploration and imaginative stories. First the child learns to handle and build with blocks and not to throw them. Then he is free to create open-ended structures. Learning to put them away is an important part of block play that is a balance of the two activities. The blocks probably go in a certain place, but the fun of putting them away, stacking them in a variety of patterns in the process, open-ended.

In the first *casa dei bambini* in Rome Dr. Montessori accepted many beautiful dolls and toys from her friends to furnish the room when it first opened. In the beginning the children played with these toys every day. But their request to do the real work was respected by Dr. Montessori. She designed small materials and tools that would fit their hands so they could join in the work of cooking and keeping themselves and the environment clean and neat, activities that their caretakers were carrying out. Then the children no longer wanted to pretend, to play with the toys, and they were removed. There was no longer a need to pretend.

This same preference for real work over make-believe has been observed all over the world for many years. In a new class of 2.5-6 year-olds one will often find familiar link-with-the-home toys such as bead stringing, puzzles, or blocks for the children to play with in the beginning of the year, while they are learning to put things away and to wait for a turn, and other basic skills. Learning to wait for one's turn is easy because there is only one of each toy, only one of each piece of educational material, in the classroom and a child is allowed to work with his choice for as long as he desires. As the children become involved with the practical life and other activities in the classroom the link-with-the-home toys are gradually removed because they are no longer being chosen.

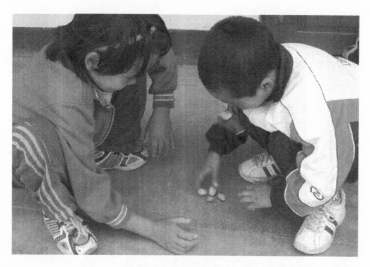

In Nepal the game of "gatti" is played with stones and has many challenging steps of throwing and catching that children love to master.

If a child is included in the regular food preparation in the family, helping to set the table, take out the compost, wash the dishes, he is not going to be interested in pretending to cut a wooden banana with a play knife, or pretending to wash plastic dishes. If children are raised without early exposure to television and computers, are used to physical movement and work, and interacting with people, at a very young age, they will have much less patience for passive entertainment later.

The most important element in selecting toys, and creating an environment for children, is to include examples that will engage the child's mental faculties for a long period of time, combining movement of the body with the work of the brain. These challenges can lead to discovery, concentration, and fun.

In the Montessori 3-6 classroom the teacher demonstrates the use of each new piece of sensorial material to a child with enthusiasm, slowly and carefully showing him how to handle the materials, and a first lesson on what to do with it. It can be the same at home. Sometimes, when it is not obvious what can be done with a toy or puzzle, or there are no older siblings or neighbors around to imitate, the adult can simply play with the toy with, or in front of, the child as an inspiration. At home as in class, the adult can watch for the moment when the child is finished and offer to help put it away, having thought out ahead of time where it might go. This prevents loss, damage, or mishandling of toys and provides the needed order in the environment. It will avoid the common nagging to put things away if the child is shown where it goes; this is an example of the saying: Teach by teaching, not by correcting.

The order and simplicity of the Montessori classroom supports the strong need for order the child has at this age. There are no toy chests or boxes of toys. Every single item in the room has a place where it belongs. The teacher and assistant constantly model the putting away unused items in their place, and the children imitate their actions. This can be done in the home, rotating toys if necessary so there are no more toys than there are simple and logical spaces for them.

As I have said, blocks are a favorite of children the world over, and are conducive in leading the child to the experience of long periods of concentration, creativity, and happiness. They can be made from simple stones, clay bricks, pieces of tree branches, or polished hardwoods. The attraction is that the imagination of the child is set free to create relationships between these physical objects, and to explore them endlessly. Many mathematical and geometric relationships and architectural concepts can be discovered, and physics principles are experienced as the structure gets too tall or too heavy. The child can also work out personal problems by play-acting with blocks, animal models, and little people. In our experience, next to doing real family work, playing with blocks has been one of the most valuable toys for a young child at home.

Puzzles provide practice in visual discrimination as the child figures out exactly how the elements fit together visually, and they support the development of eye-hand control as the pieces are fitted together. They teach the child that work/play can have a beautiful and logical structure. They more easily give practice in the beginning and ending of an activity and the satisfaction of completion. The progression of puzzles is first 1, 2, or

3 piece knobbed puzzles, then multiple-piece knobbed puzzles, simple jigsaw puzzles in frames with gradually increasing numbers of pieces, then cube puzzles and regular cardboard jigsaw puzzles.

A child is eager to learn correct use, to know the exact techniques for doing a puzzle, using a kitchen or woodworking tool, a gardening tool, or the technique of playing a musical instrument. We would be doing a child a disservice if we allowed him to use anything — blocks, a violin bow, a hand mixer — as a hammer, for example. This does not stifle creativity, but facilitates it! Playing with open-ended toys, such as dolls, blocks, art materials, and so forth, is made infinitely richer by the child's knowledge of exact techniques in handling other materials.

Through the use of toys such as these a child learns how to think, to concentrate, to follow a thought, to complete a cycle of activity, and to solve problems. He learns to use his body, especially his hands, under the control of his will, to be self-disciplined. This is the foundation for the creativity of a professional artist or composer, and for the creativity of a child at any age.

Thinking and planning games, such as chess, hold a fascination for children. Our children and grandchildren loved learning the names of the pieces, and the way they could move, at a very early age, one step at a time over months and years. Competition did not enter into it, just the fun of moving the little figures and trying to remember which piece could do what. At first we played a "pawn game" both of us having only pawns on the board and learning the rules a pawn must follow. Then we would play the same kind of game with only bishops, or knights. Then we would combine two and play a "rook-queen" game, moving each around the board in their own ways. Eventually our children, and then grandchildren, learned real chess, not competing to beat each other, but with the fun of learning all those rules and following them.

Cooperative games such as "Harvest Time" (a board game made by a family in Canada) teach children to work together, to help each other, to consider the good of the other person or the group as well as oneself, instead of fostering competition and winning. Competitive play cause players to feel isolated or left out; players are secretive and the game can result in hard feelings or arguments. After a family learns to play coop games it is possible to turn other games into coop versions. In environments where children work and play cooperatively rather than competitively, they learn the most valuable kind of socialization—helping each other. We consider this valuable preparation for positive interaction throughout life.

Preparation for later academic work: in the following pages you will find ideas for introducing the child to the world in ways that are appropriate for the stage of development he is in at the moment. We do not believe in pushing a child, but we believe strongly in providing an environment rich in all areas of learning so that the child can choose, from his own intuition, what he is ready to learn. Young children show an amazing interest in a wide range of subjects. A rich environment, full of interesting activities having to do with music, art, history, geography, science, language, and math, inspires curiosity, fosters broad interests, and extends the child's experience. Observations in homes and schools with environments such as these have taught us to focus on the preparation of an environment, at age 3-6, allowing the child to explore and learn from the environment when he is interested, rather then having an adult sit down (usually at the adult's convenience) to "teach." This allows the child to choose and to teach himself, to make intelligent choices of what to do, to repeat the activity until he is satisfied, and to concentrate. The adult's challenge is to be sure that the environment offers all the key experiences necessary for laying this foundation.

Cooperative, non-competitive, games such as "Harvest Time" create an excellent standard for playing with others. Children love angel chimes and blocks, and at this age can enjoy learning the rules of how each chess piece can move.

Rather than relying on verbal lessons given by an adult, or computers and TV, or videos (or other examples of passive learning), we provide the child with real life activities from which he will really learn and remember what he learns. We can, with planning, create an environment that is rich in experiments, games, materials, and books which the child can select as an interest arises, providing valuable experiences of the hand and mind working together for an intelligent purpose.

THE EARTH, PHYSICAL SCIENCES

*Playing in water, digging in sand, feeling the mud
between one's toes and the wind in one's face—all
of these are experiences of the physical sciences.*

*It is not enough for the teacher to restrict herself
to loving and understanding the child; she must first
love and understand the universe.*
— **Maria Montessori**

At this age we do not tell the child about the
problems with the environment, global warming, etc.
Giving this information too early can cause confusion
and stress, worry and even an avoidance of anything to
do with the earth. Instead we share the wonder and the
beauty of the earth. This is true of the studies of plants
and animals, and of people of the world. Children grow
up to care about, be interested in, and care for, the things
they have learned to love.

Interest in the study of astronomy, earth, ecology, physics, and chemistry can all begin now when the child is the most interested in new experiences, when he literally absorbs everything in the environment. The first lessons about Earth come from nature — experiences of the sun and wind, playing in sand and water and mud, seeing the sun rise and set, watching the stars at night, visiting the seashore, and from the child's own collections of rocks and minerals.

At age 3-6 we give what are called sensorial keys — such as rocks, globes, puzzle maps, landforms, pictures of the sun, moon, planets, and a few constellations and cloud formations (and only the most simple comments) to go along with the experience of these materials. We do not give long verbal explanations now, but later at the age of six or seven, when the imagination can reach back through time and through space. It is not until the age of six and beyond, when the child has a different kind of mental approach to learning, which is centered around the imagination, that we give explanations and details about the history of the solar system, and the inside of the earth, and so forth.

Because the most logical way to present information is from the general to the specific, we give the child at this age a sensorial experience of the solar system with simple mobiles and puzzles, then an exposure to a model of the earth with globes, puzzle maps, pictures, and books. Even in the homes and classrooms of the very youngest children we find an interest in solar mobiles and rock collections.

A globe is probably one of the most important pieces of material to have in the home. When a child has made lakes and rivers in the sand at the beach or in a sandbox, the parent can show him that the blue areas of the globe represent the water, the seas, and the other areas the land. This is enough to begin. In the classroom children at this early stage learn the names of the continents and they remember them because this is the age when the mind takes in everything in the environment.

With this foundation eventually the past and present meet when we look for countries where plants or literature originated (the tulips from the mountains of Asia by way of Holland, the Bible from the Middle East, for example). A globe can be referred to when friends send a postcard during a trip, or when different countries are referred to in children's books. When we eat rice with chopsticks, or tacos, or hear Irish music on the radio, we can show the child where these things came from. Puzzle maps give practice in recognizing the shapes of continents and oceans. They combine the child's need for movement and shape recognition with developing awareness of the earth.

Children love to dig in sand and mud—forming islands, lakes, peninsulas, capes, and other land and water forms, at the beach or in the garden. In class they form clay land and water forms in small pie pans. They enjoy knowing the names and pouring water and maybe floating little homemade walnut-shell boats on the lake or bay they have made.

I would like to repeat, this is not the age for focusing on all of the problems that are besetting Earth. Children at this age naturally feel a oneness with all of creation and it can cause pain or a shutting-down to tell them of problems too early. Instead we focus on their love — beauty, of caring for objects, of knowledge, and language. We give them the sensorial experiences of rocks, landforms, oceans, clouds, stars, lakes, and the visual and tactile possibilities to work with them by means of puzzle maps. And then we give the names. All of this experience and knowledge leads to a natural concern and responsibility at a later age because children "love what they know."

The earth was formed by principles inherent in simple physics and chemistry experiments. We give simple first experiments to children now in a motor-sensorial way, not with a lot of words and explanations. For example in class there is a "Sink and Float" game. It consists of 10 or more objects some of which will float and some will not. The teacher shows a child how to put out a plastic mat on a table, fill the bowl with water, test each object, and sort them into a pile of those that sink and those that float, then to dry everything, pour out the water, and put everything back in its place for the next child. This is easy to do in the home, as a game, or just casually in the bath.

We do not talk or explain this phenomenon from an adult point of view, we give no labels or language, but let the child ponder, and repeat the experiment whenever he is interested. It is not uncommon for the child to carry out the activity such as the sink and float game, carefully drying everything each time, over and over as a deep and private understanding of the physics principle grows in him. And then return to it day after day. It is only after the child has had some experience, when the actions mean something, that we introduce the terms *sink* and *float*.

A child demonstrating a simple circuit in a classroom in the Bahamas

There are other simple science materials for the child to play/work with as much as he desires, in that way absorbing the basic principles that will lead to later interest and study of earth sciences. Children at this age love working with water, magnets, batteries, candles, and other real physics materials, each a key to a basic physical law that will be internalized now and help with academic studies later in life.

Although videos and television have their place in education for older children and adults, they are not the best way to learn at this age. Imagine the difference between standing on a hill, with the wind in your face, watching the sun go down at the end of the day — and watching a sunset on a TV screen. Young children are learning with all of their senses, and experiences that are multi-sensorial stay with them for a lifetime.

Successful lessons consist in a quiet demonstration of a piece of material — a puzzle, an experiment, which can then be carried out by the child at will, as many times as there is interest. Modern brain research shows that young children use the visual and auditory parts of the brain at different times. Demonstrating and explaining an activity at the same time interrupts the ability to concentrate and focus. Dr. Montessori did not know of this brain research, but she observed over and over the difference between the attention of a child who is being shown a lesson silently, and one who was being asked to listen and watch at the same time. So when you are trying to show something to a child, how to sort objects that sink or float for example, try to refrain from talking while you are demonstrating an action, and refrain from demonstrating an action while you are speaking.

One of the most important elements of the learning process is the ability to express what one has begun to understand through art, music, language, or in some other tangible way. Children love to create original art connected to puzzle maps, and the easiest time to learn the names of continents, oceans, rivers, etc. is before age six, when a child wants to handle everything and learn what everything in his environment is called. Many of us have been astounded at the young child's ability to learn geographical terms. This is not surprising as the child under the age of six is in the strongest *sensitive period* for learning language he will ever experience. This child will learn thousands of words if he has sensorial experiences of them.

Puzzle maps, magnets, books about continents and countries, a prism—all are physical science.

Sometimes it has been said that there is not enough creativity in the Montessori class, because in a traditional school the child will be creating so many art projects. In my mind this stems from a basic misunderstanding of the meaning of "creativity." One will see drawing, painting, and clay in the Montessori environment, but everything else the child is doing, when it is of his own volition, is creative. Also, the two and three-dimensional arts are combined with all of the other studies. A child may decide to trace around puzzle pieces of the countries of South America and then paint them. Or he may make up a song or funny rhyme about favorite countries, or make a model of an animal with clay. All of the various activities are available to the children at any time of the school day and seeing how they are combined is one of the joys of being a Montessori teacher.

PLANTS AND ANIMALS, LIFE SCIENCES

At home, cleaning up the raised beds for the winter

*Solicitous care for living things affords
satisfaction to one of the most lively instincts of the
child's mind. Nothing is better calculated than this
to awaken an attitude of foresight.*
—Maria Montessori

An atmosphere of love and respect for plants and animals in the home and classroom is the best foundation for a lifetime of comfort with, and interest in, nature. This begins in the home as the child absorbs the family's attitude toward gardens, houseplants, weeds, wild birds, and pets. Lessons that make a deep impression come from first hand experiences of plants and animals; nothing can substitute for seeing, and smelling flowers in the home, and watching the daily growth of a flower or vegetable in the garden or filling a bird feeder with a parent and watching which birds come to feed.

A little "nature" table or shelf, in the home or classroom, dedicated to a changing array of beautiful objects from nature, is a delight to children. Some suggestions of what to put on it are a vase of flowers or leaves, a tray of variously colored leaves in the fall, a plant experiment, a collection of shells, "found" bird or old insect nests, and perhaps famous artwork depicting animals. It is important to keep the nature table very clean because this shows respect for nature and it attracts children to spend time with it. A little tray with a magnifying glass could be kept on the nature table for closer observation.

It is also the place where the botany experiment of planting a seed and watching it grow into a plant can be placed. When planting a seed in a little pot to observe its growth the plant in class should belong to all of the children. This is different than in some more traditional classes where each child plants his own seed in a cup. There is a good reason for this. Some seeds will sprout and others will not, some plants will grow and some will wither, just because of the variety of seeds. This can be very sad for a child to see his die when others are growing. It can make him feel that he has done something wrong. When the planted seed belongs to the whole group they will celebrate together as the seed grows, or they will grieve together if it dies.

In the 3-6 classroom a plastic mat, bucket and sponge, and a small drying towel are kept on a tray under or near the nature table. One of the favorite activities is to carefully clean the table and the items on the table. Lay on the floor a plastic mat and carefully remove everything from the table. If there are dry leaves or soil, show the child how to wipe them off the edge of the table and into his hand. Next show him how to dip and wring out the sponge, and to wipe the top of the table and the legs. With a drying cloth dry everything. Wipe and dry the plastic mat, then clean the sponge, hang the drying cloth up to dry and replace it with a fresh one. And replace the items on the table, letting the child decide on their arrangement. Now the child knows how to carry out this activity at any time, independently of an adult's permission. This gives the child the feeling of really caring for the beautiful objects and not just looking at them.

It is important for a child to spend some time in the outdoors experiencing nature every day if possible — in all kinds of weather and during all seasons. Going for a walk with a young child, if one follows the child's slow speed and unpredictable interests, can open our eyes to the world of nature like never before. Since this is the age that children want to know the names of everything (not the "why" and "how" explanation which comes later, but the names) we teach the names of plant, parts of the plant, kinds of roots and stems, parts of the root and stem, attachment of the leaf to the stem (such as alternate or opposite), any of the botanical concepts that will be learned later, as long as they are visible in the child's world, will work.

Flower arranging is an important part of the ritual of beginning the day in many classrooms and can be done at home. A selection of interesting tiny vases of different sizes and shapes, from different countries, is very nice. Just as with the cleaning of the nature table, a tray can be prepared with all of the items necessary for flower arranging: small vases, scissors to cut the flowers, a small pitcher to fill the vases and perhaps a funnel if the tops of the vases are small, and a sponge and drying cloth for cleaning up. A selection of handmade cotton, or hand-cut paper doilies makes this ritual very special. Having these flower arrangements on the kitchen, living room, or classroom tables, even if they consist of only one small flower or fern in a vase, brings the child's attention to the beauty and variety of nature as he goes through the day. Don't be surprised if all the flowers and vases end up on the same table the first time.

This is *not* the time to dissect flowers (or plants) with children! A child at this age identifies with the plant and animals in his world and can be very upset, even without our realizing it, at the destruction of a flower. Instead teach the names of flowers, the parts of a flower, the types of corollas, etc.

Grass, leaves, wildflowers, or cultivated flowers all make ideal art materials when they have been preserved in a flower press. In our home we have often kept previously dried leaves and flowers in a container next to the flower press ready for decorating birthday cards, or to include in letters.

If you are planning an outdoor environment for children at home or at school, be sure to include a space for wild specimens. Some of the best biological examples of leaf shapes, examples of rough (serrated) or smooth

Since it is the first time this child has cut and arranged flowers for his classroom in Moscow, he is getting help from a friend.

leaf margins, and so forth, can be found on wild plants such as dandelions and thistles. First we point out, invite to touch, and give the vocabulary for experiences and concepts such as orange, red, small, long, rough, smooth, bumpy, hard, and soft. This is a classification that even the beginning botanist can use. Very soon we can give more. The young child wants to know exact names of everything. Not just "flower" but "California poppy," and later, after exposure has stimulated an interest in plants, we can introduce the botanical names and further classification — such as kinds of leaf margins or flower corollas. Exposure to plants and animals initiates many important discussions that a wide vocabulary can enrich and make more satisfying.

Providing garden tools and a small wheelbarrow for the child, so that she can help to carry grass cuttings or anything else that needs to be transported, is an excellent way to involve the child with the yard work. Although the adult will often shy away from hard work, the young child will welcome important real work. This is the time to introduce gardening to children. Even one pot, inside or outside, with one plant, is better than nothing when there is no room for a large outside garden.

It is important to show the child the end, as well as the beginning, of any of these activities. Sometimes endings can be separate lessons so the child will be ready for them at the conclusion of a hard days work in the garden. For example, show the child how to hold the wooden handles with the points down when they are carried, exactly how to hold the shovel in order to carefully hang it up or place it where it belongs. If an adult is sensitive to the child's natural need for order, he will provide a place for every tool. Model the cleaning of the garden tools with a hose and brush, and the oiling of the wooden handles. Mastering these tasks give a great feeling of satisfaction, independence, and completion of a job well done.

Beautiful pictures of plants and flowers (photos, postcards, reproductions of great oil paintings) can be hung on the child's wall. You may be surprised at a child's preference for nonfiction books about nature, over make-believe, when he has been kept in touch with nature.

The attitude of respect for nature, plants and animals begins in the home and in the first years of life — spending as much time as is possible outside, in all seasons, experiencing animals in the natural world — listening to birds, collecting shells on the beach, reading about animals, learning to recognize and to name insects, fish, amphibians, reptiles, birds, mammals.

Children have a wonderful natural affinity for animals at an early age. Just as they are learning to be kind to each other, and to respect the environment in general, this is the time to show them exact ways to be kind to animals. One of the lessons I learned to give in my first training course in London was to pick up and hold a cat, paying attention to being quiet and moving slowly and carefully as one approaches the cat, speaking with a gentle voice. Finally to show a child exactly where to put his hands as he picks up the cat and gently cradles it to his chest. Children are delighted to learn the tiny details of caring for animals, and we should not expect them to automatically know how to treat animals without having had careful, hands-on lessons.

Animals are best observed free in nature to show children how they really live, who they really are. If we hang a bird feeder just outside the window and show the child how to sit quietly so that the birds won't be afraid, we provide the best way to watch birds, rather than while living in a cage. Binoculars give the child a feeling of participating in the birds' activities, and allow him to watch birds from a distance. It is surprising to see how a child can focus and become still when the interest in watching a bird has been awakened.

When an animal is going to visit the home or classroom, we must prepare, with the child, for all of the animal's needs ahead of time — comfort, exercise, food, warmth, gentle handling — and have the visit last only as long as the guest is comfortable. The consideration for the animal is more important than the satisfaction of our curiosity. In our home we kept two containers always clean and ready to receive a guest salamander or small garden snake. It takes no time at all to dig up a dandelion or another small plant, and to put it in the terrarium with a sprinkle of water for the animal to hide under for its short visit. A terrarium can be as elaborate as a ten-gallon aquarium with a wire top, or a simple jar.

The most important thing to keep in mind is that, even though it may be a short visit, the animal will need air. So if a container such as a large jar is used, be sure to show the child that there must be holes in the metal top, or show how to fasten cheesecloth on the top with a rubber band, or use a screen that one can purchase for making sprouted seeds in a mason jar. There should also be moisture but it is easy to put too much water in a container than is comfortable for the creature so we teach the children to pay special attention to this.

The visiting animal should not be in the class more than for the time it can be truly comfortable. Help the child understand that it is there just as a guest, for us to look at and appreciate, to learn about how it moves, what kinds of parts of the body it has, how it eats, and so forth. Then we thank it for visiting us and we let it go.

Nature songs, real but small gardening tools, shells and matching shell cards, fruit vocabulary cards

Hatching cocoons in the home or the classroom is a truly magical experience for the child, and there are mail-order larvae available so that this can be done safely at the correct time. Observing the life cycle of one animal, such as a butterfly or frog, is a good way to introduce the amazing phenomenon of life cycles in different animals that children will study in depth later. These lessons should be thought out ahead of time and presented slowly and carefully to the child. This shows that the adult respects the work and expects the child to be careful and to do his best.

At first the language cards of zoology should be shown when the animal is present. For example after observing a snake, show the child a set of cards of reptiles, which will include several snakes. These cards can be used simply as flash cards to learn the names. If there are two of each they can be used as matching cards, and later as cards to label when the child begins to write and read. When observing a fish, show the child the cards of the external parts of a fish. Then give the external parts of amphibians, birds, and mammals. Point out the similarities and the differences between the body parts of these animals and those of your own body or that of the child. Which animals have eyes and a mouth? Which have legs? Then the child will discover the connection between front legs and arms, and the variety of placement of ears, and all kinds of other things. Again, this is laying a foundation for later studies but in a way suited to the child in the motor-sensorial stage of development.

When working on the maps of the continents, show the child the animals that come from different parts of the world, from which continents. When looking at a globe that shows mountains and rivers, etc., show him which animals live in which biomes.

Books should be chosen carefully, the pictures real, and the text not just watered down adult text that is all too common, but with facts of interest to the child. Give a child simple picture books, beginning reading books, but also advanced reference books. Look for pictures of entire animals, with a white background, so the child can see exactly what we mean when we point to a picture and call it "tiger" (and not "tiger and rock and bushes," or the "head of a tiger.") Just as dissection of flowers is not appropriate at this age, the dissection of animals, and studying internal parts, can be fearsome to the young child. This is best put off till a later time of life. Art is connected to zoology as it is to all areas of study. Drawing or painting, or working with clay—from nature, books, real animals in the classroom, and from the imagination—are common daily events in the Montessori class and many homes. Displaying art prints containing animals is an inspiration for the child to create his own art, drawing and painting animals, in his own way.

A world puzzle map put together with a parent, first the parent does most of it, but one step at a time the child masters the task.

Madame Montessori,

Even as you, out of love for children, are endeavoring to teach children, through your numerous institutions, the best that can be brought out of them, even so, I hope that it will be possible not only for the children of the wealthy and the well-to-do, but for the children of paupers to receive training of this nature. You have very truly remarked that if we are to reach real peace in this world, and if we are to carry on a real war against war, we shall have to begin with children, and if they will grow up in their natural innocence, we won't

have to struggle, we won't have to pass fruitless idle
resolutions, but we shall go from love to love and
peace to peace, until at last all the corners of the
world are covered with that peace and love for which,
consciously or unconsciously, the whole world is
hungering.

— M. K. Gandhi, 1943

Today our world is shrinking and we are learning to cherish diversity — economic, racial, all kinds — to prepare children for living in the real world. Gandhi's desire is coming to pass. Montessorians have worked with children in small villages in Africa, with refugees in Cambodia, the Middle East, and Nepal, Tibetan refugees in India, with poor children in the United States, and in many other places.

Children living in international towns and cities around the world are very fortunate to be exposed to a melting pot of cultures. But every country also has its own unique history to be explored. The study of geography and of history revolves around the needs of all humans for such basic things as food, housing, a means of transportation, clothing, and the mental and spiritual needs for work, play, and worship. This emphasizes what we all have in common. In the early years children are given concrete examples, stories and pictures of people all over the world, in order to build a foundation in geography and history. Lessons center around how people have developed a culture because of the place where they live. How and why are the people living north of the Arctic Circle different from those living near the equator? Why do some people survive mostly on meat, others on fish, or on dates from palm trees? Where did potatoes and corn come from? This attitude provides a healthy, non-judgmental, non-ethnocentric, non-nationalistic, basis of exploration of peoples of the world.

The seeds of the study of history are given through sensorial experiences of ethnic foods and music, cultural

A cultural display in a classroom in Albania: flag, pictures, a statue of Mother Teresa, artifacts, and on the bottom shelf a traditional hat of Albania

objects, pictures, and books. Later children will build on the impressions taken in during this time of the absorbent mind, the age when they become all of the impressions taken in from the environment, to make sense of the history and the geography of the world.

The more easily available a globe and map is to a child, the more often it will be referred to and the more geography will be learned in a very simple and enjoyable way. In providing experiences for the child we move from the general view to the specific — from the whole earth to continents, to countries, to counties, then towns, and neighborhoods.

I remember one day my oldest daughter, Narda, then three years old and recently having begun attending a Montessori school, was watching me, along with some of her older friends (ages six and eight), pour some beaten eggs into a skillet. She said, "That looks like Africa!" One of the older children peeked into the pan and asked, "What is Africa?" To which Narda replied, "It is a continent." The other friend asked her what a continent was and Narda said, with a little bit of exasperation, "Come with me." She then got out the globe and sat the older girls down for a very enjoyable lesson on the names of the continents and countries of the world. There is no reason to put off geographical studies until later grades. Children want to have an idea of where they live on a globe of Earth at very young age.

Since this is the time when children love to do puzzles, and to know the names of everything in the environment, we follow the children's interests and introduce them to the world by offering geography puzzles, the continents and the countries of the world. Again, following the idea of the general to the specific, first they are given puzzles that have oceans and landmasses or continents only. Next they are introduced to a knobbed puzzle in which each piece represents a country in the child's own continent. And then, for the USA as an example, a puzzle in which each piece represents a state. Puzzle maps have been used in 3-6 classes for many years and it has been shown over and over that children at this age easily memorize the names, relative sizes, shapes, and the location of continents and countries of the world much more easily than after age six. Children delight in learning these things, as always when learning is joyful, this knowledge is likely to stay with them forever.

We also give national songs, dances, instrumental music, costumes, pictures of state birds, flowers, flags, architecture, inventions, and picture cards of adults and children carrying out the many aspects of life. We are very careful not to give the impression that any culture is superior in any way to any other. Pre-industrial countries often have social and environment aspects that have been lost to more technologically advanced countries. This is not the age to discuss this aspect of cultures, but it is important for the adult to keep this in mind because her attitudes will be a model for the child.

Flags of the world have a special attraction to children. Ideally every classroom has a set of the flags of the world, and a flag book can introduce this subject in the home. A child might come into class one morning with news about a family friend who just arrived from India. He will gather all of the objects related to India in the classroom—a folder of pictures of Asia, the map of Asia with the puzzle piece of India, maybe a brass pitcher or statue from India, the flag of India, and so on. Often other children will join in the search, and maybe remind him of a song or poem from this country.

Native American materials, international flags,
books about people, and an Earth flag

Biographies of famous and not-famous people are important pieces of the puzzle that will create the child's ultimate understanding of the history of the world. The adult begins this with stories about himself, what was life like "when I was a little boy". One story I was asked to repeat over and over, when I was teaching children from age 2-6 in Montessori classes, was about the experience of getting up one morning, going through the living room to fix breakfast, and seeing our horse staring in the living room window at us. How we all laughed then went outside and led the horse back to the barn. That was all, no plot, just a true experience, and the children loved it. Telling true stories is more interesting at this age, when children want to learn about the real world, than make believe stories. Then it is an easy and important transition to tell stories about famous people when they were young. For example tell the story of Albert Einstein who didn't like to tie his shoes. This leads quite naturally to an interest in famous people of the world, and to history in general.

Singing and dancing is still common in many cultures. This little boy is singing a Tibetan song accompanied by his father.

If you can walk, you can dance. If you can talk, you can sing.

— **Zimbabwe Proverb**

Humans are born to sing. As the infant focuses on the mouth of the mother he is studying how lips move and how sounds are made. When he begins to make intentional sounds and the adult imitates them, the first duet is born. Let us help the child continue with this joyful human creation. There is no such thing as a nonmusical child; and it may be that we all could be musical adults had we been encouraged, or exposed to singing when we were children. We do not need beautiful voices to model singing for children. They will not judge us.

Songs give children a way of expressing emotions, and the very act of singing is a physical release. I have always watched for the spontaneous singing in class, knowing that it is a positive sign that the day is going well for that child when he bursts into song seemingly unaware that he is doing so. In our home, hearing our son sing in bed as he went to sleep at night was a reassuring sign that his life was in balance. Singing also gives practice in language, new words, poetry, and historical and other cultural information. In a Montessori class, where children learn and work individually instead of by means of group lessons, the teacher will sing a song, make music, dance, at any time during the day with two or three children who aren't busy. Others may join in as they please. Quite often it is the child who initiates singing and playing a percussion instrument or dancing, instead of an adult, because any child is free to make music whenever he feels the urge.

> *What does not exist in the cultural environment will not develop in the child.*
> —Dr. Shinichi Suzuki, founder of the Suzuki method of music education.

Just as beautiful speech comes from years of listening, music appreciation and accomplishment comes from years of listening to music. Songs, folk, ethnic, and classical music played on real instruments, experimentation with good percussion instruments, ideally are all a part of the life of every child. We can help a musical ear's development by being careful to eliminate background sound — TV, radio, constant random music — so that the sense of hearing is ever alert and not "turned off" by too much auditory input.

Stories of composers, especially stories about when they were children, are always interesting to young children. They show that famous composers did not just spring full-grown into being, but were regular children who were usually exposed to music as children, and later became interested in writing down the music in their heads.

> *It is important for children to realize that music is always the result of body movements. Even if there are natural sounds, children need to understand that music is produced by human beings using various muscles of the mouth, hands, and arms. They should know how many different instruments there are and should have the opportunity to witness how musicians control their gestures so as to obtain different musical sounds.*
> — **Silvana Montanaro, MD,** *Understanding the Human Being*

To help a child experience a broad base of music, we recommend providing real percussion instruments from different countries of the world, as well as inviting friends or visiting musicians who can demonstrate folk or classical instruments into the home or classroom. Listening to a heartbeat with a stethoscope, then tapping out the rhythms of the children's names (Jennifer = x x x, Alex = x x) with the instruments is a good introduction to rhythm. Children at this age are very open to learning the techniques of instruments considered very difficult—such as piano or violin—when they have a system of learning, such as Suzuki, which bases its teaching on the natural development of children.

> *A new form of educational system will not appear until we give serious consideration to the fact that we have a "double mind." Children at any age must be offered a balanced experience of verbal and intuitive thinking to help develop the great potential of the human mind. The results will not only include better functioning of the brain but also greater happiness in personal and social life.*
>
> *In Western education, we tend to separate them, because many of the things the right hemisphere (intuitive) is able to do are not highly valued in our civilization. So from a very young age, children learn not to express themselves completely with that hemisphere because they haven't been urged to give much importance to body-movement in dancing or in singing, drawing . . . all the arts. In Eastern*

civilizations, however, greater importance tends to be given to the intuitive part of the brain; the logical hemisphere is considered irrelevant in solving the real problems of our existence. It is a source of great hope for our immediate future that the most advanced human beings of both cultures are uniting in the recognition that we need each other to become complete and that we have a lot to share.
— **Silvana Montanaro, MD,** *Understanding the Human Being*

Working with clay, as in this school in the Bahamas, is soothing and satisfying for any child.

Children benefit from having a variety of art materials available to them at all times and a space to work, uninterrupted, when they are inspired. It is important to provide the best quality that we can afford — pencils, crayons, felt pens, clay, paper, and brushes — because the child will be more successful if the materials are of good quality. And the adult can model and show carefully to use and care for these things.

Individual artwork connected with other subjects is more creative, noncompetitive, and successful than group projects or models created by the teacher for children to imitate. Children should not learn to imitate the creations of an adult, to turn out products that all look alike. They should be shown carefully how to get out the clay, for example, to use each of the tools, to form basic coils and slabs. They can be introduced to clay sculptures in museums and books. In the classroom it is the child, not the teacher, who will decide when to work on clay, and exactly what to make.

Aboriginal rhythm sticks from Australia, time to dance, original drawings instead of coloring books or outlines to fill in, and art cards to introduce the best of art from the past and the present

Just as any work in the 3-6 class, each art activity is kept complete and ready for use. If a child is interested in painting for example, he will find an apron, paper, paints and brushes, all clean and ready. After watching a seed grow into a plant a child might be inspired to draw, to make leaf rubbings, a clay sculpture of a plant, or to paint the leaf or plant. Building with blocks, visiting a museum, listening to or making music, eating ethnic food, any activity can lead naturally to an artistic creation by the child.

> *The truth is that when a free spirit exists, it has to materialize itself in some form of work, and for this the hands are needed. Everywhere we find traces of men's handiwork, and through these we can catch a glimpse of his spirit and the thoughts of his time. The skill of man's hand is bound up with the development of his mind, and in the light of history we see it connected with the development of civilization.*
> — **Maria Montessori**

Reproductions of great masterpieces, as prints, cards, or in books, inspire an appreciation of beauty at any age. Hang the pictures at the child's eye level, and provide art postcards to sort into groups, such as by artist, or subjects to be found in the artistic creations, such as animals or shoes. Stories about artists, especially as children, are interesting even at this age. Good art books can engage a child for hours. At home or in the classroom, we can designate a "museum table" or a museum shelf where beautiful art objects can be placed as a temporary art exhibit, sometimes to look at and not to touch, especially if the museum table is to prepare children for visiting real museums where they will not be allowed to touch. Since everything else in the room is available for handling, this gives practice in just looking, as in a real museum, and allows close exposure to special items and beautiful objects that the child might not otherwise have. This also introduces the idea that most "art" objects in museums were used in daily life, soup bowls, jewelry, tools, and other useful and decorative creations. Whenever possible we give the best examples of art and the best art materials, at the youngest, most impressionable age.

Art is essential in the environment of the child from birth on. It is a way of approaching life, of moving and speaking, of decorating a home and school, of selecting toys and books. It cannot be separated from every other element of life. We cannot "teach" a child to be an artist, but we can help him develop, in the words of Maria Montessori:

> *An eye that sees*
> *A hand that obeys*
> *A soul that feels*

LANGUAGE

*This beautiful book corner is in a
classroom in the United States.*

*This simpler
one is in a
classroom in
Bhutan. A
child just needs
an inviting and
quiet place to curl up and look at books.*

It was very hard for me to learn how to read. It
did not seem logical for the letter "m" to be called
"em," and yet with some vowel following it you did
not say "ema" but "ma." It was impossible for me to
read that way. At last, when I went to the
Montessori school, the teacher did not teach me the

names of the consonants but their sounds. In this
way I could read the first book I found in a dusty
chest in the storeroom of the house. It was tattered
and incomplete, but it involved me in so intense a
way that Sara's fiancé had a terrifying premonition
as he walked by: "Damn! This kid's going to be a
writer."
— Gabriel Gárcia Márquez, Nobel Prize recipient
for literature

The main influence on the development of a child's spoken and written language is the family. If the adult speaks clearly and precisely to the child, and in a normal tone of voice that one would use with a peer, the child will do the same. If the child is exposed to more than one language in the home or school it is very important that he be able to associate one language with one person, and the second language with a different person. So, for example, the first adult should speak *only* English to the child, and the second adult should speak *only* Spanish to him. This will help the child sort out the difference and become fluent in both.

Reading aloud to a child gives the message that reading is fun, introduces vocabulary that would not usually come up in spoken language, and demonstrates beauty and variety of expression. Reading and writing are not "taught," in the traditional way one thinks of in learning literacy, to a child before age six or seven. Rather, the environment is prepared with sensorial experiences that will enable the child to teach himself. This was one of the most amazing discoveries of Dr.

Montessori in that very first school. Here is a quote from Dr. Montessori about her experience in the first *casa dei bambini*, "house of children," in Rome in the beginning of the 20th century:

Ours was a house for children, rather than a real school. We had prepared a place for children where a diffused culture could be assimilated from the environment, without any need for direct instruction.... Yet these children learned to read and write before they were five, and no one had given them any lessons. At that time it seemed miraculous that children of four and a half should be able to write, and that they should have learned without the feeling of having been taught.

We puzzled over it for a long time. Only after repeated experiments did we conclude with certainty that all children are endowed with this capacity to absorb culture. If this be true — we then argued — if culture can be acquired without effort, let us provide the children with other elements of culture. And then we saw them 'absorb' far more than reading and writing: botany, zoology, mathematics, geography, and all with the same ease, spontaneously and without getting tired.

And so we discovered that education is not something that the teacher does, but that it is a natural process which develops spontaneously in the human being. It is not acquired by listening to words, but in virtue of experiences in which the child acts on his environment. The teacher's task is not to talk, but to prepare and arrange a series of motives for cultural activity in a special environment made for the child.

My experiments, conducted in many different countries, have now been going on for forty years (Ed. Now 100-plus years), and as the children grew up parents kept asking me to extend my methods to the later ages. We then found that individual activity is the one factor that stimulates and produces development, and that this is not more true for the little ones of preschool age than it is for the junior, middle, and upper school children.

For success in language a child needs to feel that what he has to say is important; he needs to have a desire to relate to others; he needs to have had real experience on which language is based; and he of course needs the physical abilities necessary for reading and writing. There are several things that we can do to help. We can stop what we are doing whenever possible, listen attentively and with eye contact, and speak to the child in a respectful tone. We can provide a stimulating environment, rich in sensorial experiences and in language — language is meaningless if it is not based on experience. We can set an example and model precise language in our everyday activities with the child. If we share good literature, in the form of rhymes, songs, poetry, and stories we will greatly increase the child's love of language.

The most important first vocabulary at this age is of items in the home environment—clothing, kitchen objects, tools, toys, and so forth. Your child will be thrilled to know the names of the things he sees and uses every day, and to be able to use them correctly. All we need to do is to use the correct names, and the precise language for objects and activities, in the presence of the child. Eventually, as he joins us more in conversation, the words of the child's environment will be there.

In any good language environment, in as many situations as possible, the teacher makes sure that experience precedes vocabulary and pictures of objects. She will introduce real vegetables before vegetable cards, real actions before verb cards, real music before composer picture and labels, real shells before shell cards, and so on. At home parents can do the same thing—show the kitchen objects, the office or bathroom objects, and then give the opportunity to handle these objects and to learn the names. In this way the child learns that language is connected to the real world.

If you ever visit a Montessori classroom you will notice that there are many vocabulary books and cards. It is natural that, during this intense interest in words, children be given pictures of everything—to practice and improve their new abilities. These books and cards are valuable for the home as well.

A rich and enjoyable vocabulary, and an interesting introduction to the structure of English, is available through poems, finger plays, songs, fables, stories, and even great literature. There is only so much time in a day for reading to children so we should make the best of these times by selecting books with care, books that will provide the best in literature and nonfiction available.

Even in these early years, we give the language as we present the objects and activities that lay the foundation for many future academic studies. Give the correct names for the toys a child plays with, the colors and shapes of blocks, the parts of a broom or mop, activities such as wash, sweep, pound, pour; adjectives such as hot and cold, loud and soft; give the names of the planets, rocks, and continents; give the names of flowers, the fruits and vegetables of the home, the colors of leaves in the fall, shells, fossils, animals of all kinds, and dinosaur models; give the names of flags, famous people, countries and states; give the names of musical instruments of the world, famous paintings, artists and musicians; give the names of plane and solid shapes, counting systems in several languages, measurement terms. And this is just the beginning. Look around your own home and classroom for the elements that make your particular environments unique, and find the objects, activities, and vocabulary that you can share with children. Never again in life will the taking in of the vocabulary of the world as interesting and easily absorbed as in the first six years of life.

There are three main areas where we can help children prepare for reading and writing. When the ground is well prepared over the years before writing and reading are attempted, acquiring these skills is very enjoyable.

1) *Physical Skills* — balance, using the hands, coordination of eye-hand work, learning to concentrate and focus on practical life activities, recognizing sizes and shapes, working with knobbed puzzles, crayons and pencils, and practice in speaking.

2) *Mental Skills* — absorbing and using language, learning the *sounds* that each letter makes (not the *names* of the letter) and playing games to break up words into sounds — the "I spy" game.

3) *Social Skills* — living in homes where people talk at the table, sit down and have conversations, and read, instead of watching television or "learning language" on a computer.

The "I Spy" game: In the home or classroom when a child knows the names of objects in pictures, introduce the I Spy Game. Pick up an object, a ball. Say "I spy something in my hand that begins with b." (Make the short "b" sound, as in "tub," not the sound of the name of the letter "bee." And make it very clear what you are referring to)." Do this with several objects, maybe the same ones for weeks. Than put out two objects he has done before with different beginning sounds. "I spy something that begins with sss," the choice being between a spoon and a fork. Help him always succeed, gradually including more and more objects, "I am thinking of something in the kitchen that begins with rrr." (refrigerator). Later go on to sound out the ending sound "Something that begins with p and ends with n" (pen). Then, finally the whole word "Please hand me the "p-e-n-s-l" (pencil). Some children will move quickly to this "guessing game" and be able to guess the words you are sounding out. This is a stage very close to being able to read. This game is similar to spelling, but we say isolated sounds, not letters. "Lamb" for example would be sounded out as l-a-m. "Apple" would sound like a-p-l. And "bread" would be sound out this way b-r-e-d. This is not spelling or reading, but just exploring the sounds, individually and together in words. It is a vital and enjoyable exploration of sounds of language. You will be amazed at the ability of a child to later decode words, writing, and reading, when he has had this preparation.

Children should never be forced to read aloud, or to write, at a young age. But the tools to learn these skills provided, offered, demonstrated. This is the sensitive period in a child's life for knowing the names of everything, including the sounds of letters, and for touching and feeling. To meet the child's need to touch and feel, and to learn the names of the sounds in his particular culture, we use sandpaper letters. The child feels and says the sound, repeating many times. The traditional sandpaper letters used in the 3-6 class are very sturdy and expensive, but it is possible to make some at home, or for the child to trace letters in corn meal or sand. Sometimes one can find a book that gives this tactile experience.

Since 99 per cent of what the child will be reading is written in lower case letters, you will be doing the child a great favor to begin with these ("a" and "b," not "A" and "B"), and by giving only the sounds instead of the names of the letters. Introducing capital letters too early can make the learning both reading and writing take much longer than necessary. For those who were not physically ready to hold a pencil and write, but who were mentally ready, Dr. Montessori prepared cutout movable letters for their work. Movable alphabets, usually in cursive because they flow more easily and are easier to trace, are still used in schools today. Refrigerator magnets of lower case letters can offer this experience in the home.

When cursive sandpaper letters are used, along with ALL of the joyful pre-writing preparation that comes before the letters are introduced, writing like this is not uncommon, even by age 6.

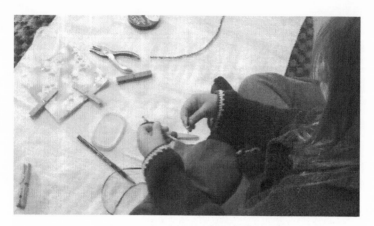

In a classroom in California, children have learned to use real book-making techniques to bind their own books.

When prepared by means of the I spy game and sandpaper lower case letters, children sometimes spontaneously "explode" into writing, and almost always "write" for a long time before they spontaneously read. This is not writing as we usually think of it, with correct spelling, space between words, correct grammar, but it is a first experience of expressing oneself with letters with great joy and enthusiasm. It is very important the child's first "writing" is from her own head, and not from objects and pictures. In fact one of the first "writings" done by a child in one of my classes was, "dontuchthiswrk iewilbeeritebak" (Don't touch work, I will be right back). I got the message.

To prepare for this experience verbally, ask questions like "What did you have for breakfast?" or "What did you see on the way to school?" Then when the child is ready to "write" with movable alphabet you can ask the same questions. Do *not* begin with easy three-letter words, or give pictures of objects with simple words, such as *hat* and *cat*, for the child to make. Written language, just as spoken language, should come from the child's own experience and desire to express himself.

Practicing letter formation in sand, books about REAL things, lower case letters only, and by age 6 books with more fantasy, all support the child's developing language abilities.

When a child first begins to recognize the sounds of letters in groups — words — he is doing this silently in his head. Saying these words aloud complicates the process, especially if someone is listening. So a child is *never* asked to *read aloud* at this early state of reading in the 3-6 Montessori class. To provide practice with this new, exciting single-word skill, give the child pictures with separate labels for objects for which he already knows the names. He reads each label and matches it to the picture. Then, if the names of the objects have been written on the back of the picture cards, the child can turn the pictures over to see if he has placed the labels correctly. Children love reading and checking their own work and will repeat over and over again till they get it exactly right. Hundreds of meaningful words can be added to the child's reading vocabulary in this way. Just as with giving spoken vocabulary, the most important words to give the child when beginning to read are the labels of the common objects in the home or classroom.

Just as the child has been taught the names of vocabulary card images before being asked to read them (silently) the first early reading books should have been read to the child, by an adult or older child, many times before he is expected to read them (silently) for himself. These days there are wonderful books available covering real subjects in the child's world—parts of the flower, kinds of tools, islands and lakes, children doing real things, kinds of musical instruments—in simple yet interesting language. Above all, this early introduction of the world or language must be offered in a spirit of enjoyment and not imposed. We have to put behind us memories of the painful way most of us learned to read and write and enjoy the joy of discovery children experience when language is given to them in this way.

Geometry, Math, and Measurement

The study of the development of the Roman Arch in later years is introduced at this age as a simple puzzle constructed of small wooden blocks.

If men had used only speech to communicate their thought, if their wisdom had been expressed in words alone, no traces would remain of past generations. It is thanks to the hand, the companion of the mind, that civilization has arisen. The hand has been the organ of this great gift that we inherit.
—Maria Montessori

I do not know when geometry and mathematics became a study I dreaded, but I do remember when I started enjoying it. My father loved math and enjoyed explaining the operation of the slide rule to me. He wanted very much to have someone in the family who shared this passion; there was no one. In school math was required, the multiplication tables were essential and painful, and even some teachers hated teaching math as much as some students hated learning it. Then, during my Montessori 3-6 training, I observed schools where children chose math over everything else and worked on it for hours and hours, and where teachers loved teaching it! I found this to be the case when I was teaching Montessori. Later, in teaching Montessori 6-12 classes I saw the same love of math with square root, cubing, algebra, math bases, all areas of math. It was through the experience of teaching Montessori that I myself learned to find enjoyment, awakened curiosity, in every subject. More and more I then could pass on a true love of learning to my students.

The concepts of math and geometry as symbols on paper make sense after the early sensorial experiences in early life. When math and geometry are disconnected from real objects, taught only with pencil and paper, these studies become dry and meaningless. Children naturally have an interest in all aspects of mathematics, weight, order, systems, series, time, quantities, and symbols, and so forth. We can serve the development of the mathematical mind by feeding this interest, giving sensorial experiences first, and only later the representatives on paper.

Sometimes people think there is something magic about sensorial math materials. Yes, the materials are certainly ingenious, but the real value of manipulatives is that they support the natural curiosity about math concepts and activities that naturally exist in us. The materials are simple and clear; there are no counting bunnies or balloons that confuse the child. Math activities include: counting, weighing and measuring, the decimal system, fractions, multiplication and division, and more. The child has been prepared for this work by carrying out real everyday activities such as dish washing with its many sequential and logical steps, matching colors, sorting, classifying objects, carrying heavy and light objects, and many other physical, sensorial activities that nourish the mathematical mind.

When the first *casa dei bambini* in Rome was opened in the beginning of the 20th century the children were not taught math. The parents asked Dr. Montessori if, now that their children were obviously loving to read and write, if she could teach them math. She had developed math for the children in the 6-12 classes but not the 3-6 classes. When she saw that the 3-6 children themselves were asking to use the math materials from the elementary classes she offered them to the younger children. She found that the younger children were often more successful at learning these concepts than the older children. From then on math became an important part of Children's Houses for children from the age of three to six.

Some people however misunderstand the teaching of math at such an early age. It is probably the case that these parents or educators are remembering their own experience with the subject. They remember how they learned the multiplication tables for example—tedious and boring, hours of painful repetition that was certainly not the first choice of activities. On the other hand there are parents who love math and are thrilled that there is an enjoyable way for their children to learn this subject. In the 3-6 class, children love to learn the quantities and symbols for numbers in the units, tens, hundreds, thousands, and millions. They often learn addition, subtraction, multiplication, and division with the decimal system and with fractions, simultaneously. None of this work is required of the children, but it is offered, presented with manipulative materials to one child at a time, by means of lessons given by the adult and sometimes by another child. There are no teachers lecturing to a group of children who are required to sit still and listen. The children choose this work, and repeat each step with joy and enthusiasm until they are ready to move to the next step.

Certainly not every child masters, or even works with, every piece of math material in a 3-6 class. The main point is that an enjoyable and interesting introduction to all of the areas of geometry and math is present in the environment. The child is introduced to each activity, as he is ready, and given the choice of whether or not to continue to work with it. In the meantime, he is aware of other children joyfully exploring math in all its variety. Math and geometry are presented and treated in the same way as art, building with blocks, music, gardening, and all other subjects. A child who is allowed to explore with real mathematical objects at an early, motor-sensorial, age stands a good chance of becoming a real math lover later in life. If his passions lie elsewhere, at least he will be exempt from the math phobia that some of us experience because of our own less-than-joyful introductions to this area of learning.

In the above pictures one can see:

1) An example of the discoveries in color and shape make by playing with geometry blocks

2) The joy of making one's own freehand shapes rather than tracing

3) One of many books used to introduce the differences in math around the world

4) A classroom in Tanzania where all of the Montessori materials were made from "found" objects, and they worked fine.

In the home or in Montessori classes in areas of the world where purchasing the expensive beads and other math materials one finds in many classrooms is not viable, they can be made of cardboard cubes, strings of beads, blocks, and beans, anything that helps the child grasp the concept through his senses. In fact, the more one uses everyday objects for comparing, measuring, counting, and carrying out any other mathematical processes, the more likely it is that mathematical exploration will become a part of the real, practical, everyday life of the child.

PART TWO, AGE 6-12

TRANSITION TO THE ELEMENTARY YEARS

Although academics and sports are important, the feeling of worth resulting from hauling and stacking firewood for the winter cannot be rivaled.

This child nearing age six or seven is passing beyond what is known as the sensory-motor developmental stage, when movement and exploration through the senses is a basic need in all learning. Now he will gradually move to a more cerebral exploration, giving up the manipulative materials according to his personal timetable. The years from 6-12 are relatively stable, and the main academic work can be done now. However it is important that the child continues to use his body as well as his mind, to get exercise, to begin to learn about and take responsibility for nutrition and health, and to continue practical work such as cooking, gardening, working with tools. Well-grounded healthy habits begun now will go a long way to help the child through the tumultuous years of adolescence. And above all we must remember that the basis of all of the 6-12 work was laid in the first six years of the child's life.

It is true that now is a good time for academic work because a child is mentally, physically, and emotionally stable. At home the parent often says, "You concentrate on your homework and I will do the dishes (or mow the lawn or carry in the groceries, or weed the garden or...)." Even the teacher thinks, "Academics is the most valuable use of your time. Other people can wash the windows, shovel the snow, shop for food and prepare meals, do the school laundry, etc. " How then is this child going to practice the skills of taking care of himself, taking care of others, taking care of the environment? What could be more important at this very social and moral age? How is he, in our modern world, expected to spend his non-academic time when he is never included in the real work of the family, the group? Too often he will be expected to spend his time being entertained — play dates, TV, shopping, texting, *hanging out*. How valuable is this child to his family and friends, and how does it make him feel about his value as a human being? This is not a balanced life. Not a meaningful life. Not a useful life. What message does this give to the child? It tells him that, for six years, he is expected only to study and to play, not to engage in any socially useful work. Academic studies are very important, but when a child's self-image is completely dependent on how he does academically, and when all of his non-academic time is spent on himself, this is not good.

In pre-industrial societies where children are still able to participate in real life every day, there are no terms such as "pre-teen" or "teenager," because these children, from the time they can walk to the time they graduate from school, have been valuable, contributing, respected, and useful members of the family, of the community. Their years from 12-18 are not separated from the rest of life as a problem period of life. They feel useful and valued, and they develop the skills that will help them become mature and responsible adults, husband, wives, fathers, and professionals. As West meets East, TV and compulsory education are taking their toll in these mostly pre-industrial countries, and a balance must be found. But industrial societies can learn from pre-industrial societies. And the reverse is also true. Let us hope that together we can find a balance for the children at this stage of life.

At six, there is a great transformation in the child, like a new birth. The child wants to explore society and the world, to learn what is right and wrong, to think about meaningful roles in society. He wants to know how everything came to be, the history of the universe, the world, humans and why people behave the way they do. He asks the *big* questions and wants answers. These children explore manners (both good and bad manners!) and will try out various behaviors at home to see how the parents react, to find out what is acceptable and what is not. They are interested in religion and what it means to people in different cultures. It is the time to use the mind to explore all areas of knowledge, to begin to conduct research, and to develop creative ways of processing, exploring, and expressing this knowledge.

A Montessori elementary teacher has spent many months learning to give individual lessons in all academic areas, and to guide the child's research. Although groups form spontaneously, the main work is still done individually — concentration protected from interruptions by group lessons — the hallmark of Montessori education at any age. These periods of deep concentration heal and fulfill a child, revealing the true human who naturally exhibits the desire to work, help others, and make a difference in the world. The period from 6-12 is sometimes known as the "social" age, but this does not mean that children are free to talk all day long. Yet sometimes one finds this to be the case in Montessori elementary classes. I remember the story of Margaret Stephenson, our wonderful and wise British Montessori teacher trainer, visiting a 6-12 class here in the USA. It was one of the classes where, unfortunately, there was a constant stream of chatter. She took it just as long as she could and then this lovely and well-mannered woman stood up and called out, "Be quiet!" I am sure the teacher of that class learned her lesson that day. I do recommend this; it only worked because Miss

Stephenson was known for her sense of humor as well as her wisdom and knowledge.

In my own 6-12 classes I have noticed that some children need absolute silence in order to concentrate, while others seem to be unaware of the talking going on around them and are still able to do their individual work, to concentrate deeply. So in each different place where I taught I arranged, with the help of the children, an area where talking was prohibited and an area where it was allowed. It was interesting to see that the needs of different groups were different, some year the group was made up of mostly those who needed silence, and other year it was the opposite, and so the size of the designated areas also changed. These individual needs must be taken into account in creating an environment where learning can take place.

Many teachers and Montessori teacher trainers see more benefits to the child when they experience the full 6-12-age span in one class. Teachers get to know the children better, there is more peer-teaching, and students are exposed to an incredible variety of work at all levels from the very beginning. Others prefer to split the ages into 6-9 and 9-12, and of course this is necessary when the teacher had had only 6-9 or 9-12 training.

According to the writings of Dr. Montessori, the suggested age span is *at least* three years, but she emphasized that there should be open doors, and free flow of children from the 3-6, 6-9, and 9-12 rooms if they have been divided into these age groupings, perhaps by law. Camilla Grazzini, the long-time Montessori 6-12 trainer in Italy, and his wife Baiba remind us, in the AMI "Communications I, 2003" and again in "Communications 2010 Special Issue," that we must make this decision based on psycho-pedagogical reasons, not the practical, financial, or scheduling, reasons of a school. They say that if the children are split into 6-9 and 9-12 classes, that in each class there should be a full set of materials for the full 6-12 age span, so that the children are completely free to work at their own pace in all of the areas of the curriculum. In my experience I can definitely see the wisdom in this, as it is quite common for a 7-year-old to do 11-year-old work and vice versa. And it would be very rare for a child, without pressure or requirements of the adult, to complete every lesson in every area of the curriculum at the 6-9 level before moving on. There should be instead an atmosphere of peace and steady progress. The teacher's role is to inspire the child to want to do research, to learn more. It is *not* to require and "teach." As my 6-12 trainer, Margaret Stephenson often reminded us "The teacher is in charge of the minimum, the child the maximum."

There are two parts to the curriculum at this age. The first is the list of basic requirements set by the state or country where the school exists. The second is the Montessori curriculum. It is the responsibility of the teacher to find out the state/country requirements and to make it available to the students.

Unlike traditional schools the teacher does not impose specific work, or homework, but instead inspires the child to want to know more! The list of state requirements, by year, is made available for the child but this, I have found, takes less than 1/3 of the child's time. The teacher meets with each child periodically, perhaps weekly in the beginning for the first year, to discuss how to meet these requirements and balance this with the other areas of work. Together they make a list, but the child learns to be in charge. This teaches time-management skills, and responsibility for one's own work. There are many different ways to help the child meet the state or country requirements, and to help him make plans and keep track of the usually much more interesting and exciting non-required work. Above all the teacher must watch out for the tendency to make assignments, to divide the day, the week, the year, into scheduled work periods and projects, to fall back on the way most of us were educated. This is very destructive to the whole idea of Montessori.

This does *not* mean to abandon the child. She watches carefully to discover the learning style of each child, and to help him reach, not just the minimum, but the highest level of work and accomplishment in each area of the curriculum each child chooses to master at any one time.

There are many ways to keep track of work and progress at this period of development, but the more the child is in charge of keeping records the better. In my classes there was a graph on a clipboard in each area of the classroom where children could check off the lessons he had had been given and then had mastered, the physics experiments or noun lessons for example. That way not only could a child see what he needed to do next, but he could see who of his friends had mastered that lesson, so he could go to that friend for the lesson instead of waiting till I had time to give it to him.

Miss Stephenson told us that if a child is having trouble getting down to work, the teacher can show him how to temporarily keep a daily journal, recording his work and the time each project is begun and completed, in order for the child to become aware of how his time is being spent. As the child discovers the problem he gets busy again, and no journal is needed, as it would be an impediment to the creative flow so evident in Montessori elementary education, the "being in the moment" that the neuroscientist Adele Diamond says is so necessary for true creativity.

The main 6-12 work is built around the five great lessons given at the beginning of each year for the new students. They introduce: the creation of earth, the coming of plants and animals, the arrival of humans, the development and spread of language, and also math and invention. In some Montessori 6-12 courses a 6th great lesson, the great river, presents a framework for the history of human cooperation, laying the groundwork for teaching an understanding of social cooperation and solidarity in the classroom. These lessons are designed by the teacher and include stories, pictures, and other experiments, charts, and activities. Many older children attend, revisiting the lessons from a new perspective, experiencing them differently each year depending upon their own growth in understanding.

For example, timelines are made with long strips of fabric or paper on which the child lays out fossils or pictures of dinosaurs on the timeline of life, and composer and musician pictures, etc. on the timeline of human civilizations, to get a visual picture of history in each subject. All work is interwoven with art, music, math, and many other creative projects, pulled together as a self-appointed group of students work together to create a presentation that they give in front of any students in the class who are interested.

The follow-up work of the five great lessons lasts throughout the child's years in the class. The discoveries related to each great lesson develop parallel to each other, the students moving back and forth from history, biology, music, language, geometry, and all of the areas of study, and they discover that all learning is ultimately related. Each year the children, as they grow older, delve deeper and deeper into the many lessons of the basic curriculum, sometimes going places that none of us expected, and so teaching us adults, to also appreciate knowledge in a new way.

What good is knowledge if it is not combined with consideration for others? Peace is not studied as an independent subject, but with the study of examples from the past, and practice in serving food, caring for, and helping each other. Peace is the natural outcome of a method of education where children experience work with their hands and minds working together, for long periods of individual concentration and contemplation. In this way they are able to process and recover from all the input of our modern world. They learn that peace is not just the absence of war, but it is the way we feel inside, in the way we treat each other in our daily lives, the way we communicate, and the way we solve problems. Children learn from experience, that peace begins inside a person, at home, at school.

> *The acts of courtesy which he has been taught with a view to his making contacts with others must now be brought to a new level. The question of aid to the weak, to the aged, to the sick, for example, now arises. If, up to the present, it was important not to bump someone in passing, it is now considered more important not to offend that person. While the younger child seeks comforts, the older child is now eager to encounter challenges. But these challenges must have an aim. The passage to the second level of education (age 6-12) is the passage from the sensorial, material level to the abstract. A turning toward the intellectual and moral sides of life occurs at the age of seven.*
>
> **— Maria Montessori**

THE EARTH, PHYSICAL SCIENCES

*This child has set himself the task of painting the
countries of the continents of the world,
exemplifying, "The teacher is in charge of the
minimum, the child the maximum."*

What is the meaning of the *cosmic task* that one hears
so much about at this stage of education? There is today
a social movement to bring the spiritual view of life and
sciences back together. We can help by giving lessons
that show the child that all of the rules of physics and
chemistry (e.g. gravity, heat rising, the rules of the
combining of substances) follow an order dictated by a
creative force or logic. They learn that each element,
from the tiniest atom to the human being, has an
important role to play, a *cosmic task*, in this scheme of
life. The term *cosmic task* is used often in the elementary
class. Cosmos is the opposite of chaos, and implies some

kind of a logical order to reality, and children at this age are fascinated by attempts to figure it out.

Dr. Montessori pointed out that every participant in our world has some important task to perform, a task that will fulfill a need for itself, and in the process contribute to the need of others. She used what she understood about the life of the common mollusk as an example. As it draws calcium carbonate out of the seas to build its protective coating, its house or shell, the mollusk at the same time, reduces the level of this potentially toxic substance from seawater. If the level of this mineral were high enough it would have a negative effect all life on earth. She explained this as the *cosmic task* of the mollusk, the role of helping itself and the planet by the same effort. Another example that children find fascinating is that of the lowly common fly that lays its eggs on dead creatures, its offspring devour the tissues, feeding themselves, and at the same time ridding the environment of dead matter that would otherwise pile up and pollute the earth; this is the cosmic task of the fly. An artist, in fulfilling an inner command to express through paints a feeling that must get out and can be expressed in no other way, brings beauty and/or meaning to others sometimes throughout generations. This is the *cosmic task* of the artist. Children explore first the cosmic task of the elements found on Earth and active during the formation of the Earth's crust, then the way living creatures provide for their own needs as they contribute to the well-being of others, and finally humans. As a result of this process a child realizes that he also has an important part to play in life, and he begins an internal inquiry of his own possible contribution and path through life.

Lessons follow a path that leads from the general to the specific, from the simple to the complex. As in all areas of the elementary curriculum, earth sciences— physics, chemistry, and so on, begin with the overview and progress to details. The child learns the functioning of the galaxies, the universe, then solar systems, the formation of Earth, seasons, natural wonders, the weather, rocks and minerals, etc. As he learns about the discoveries in the past he participates in present discovery by means of experiments and research in all areas. Beginning at age six, physics, chemistry, geography, and so on are introduced and continue until the end of the elementary class at age twelve. Older children often come to lessons given to the younger children, and younger children are welcome at lessons given to their elders. Each year the child sees more interrelatedness between these areas because lessons and experiments are going on all the time, in all academic areas at all levels. This repetition leads to deeper understanding as the child incorporates his own ever-changing and deepening experience. Because the child at this age has an active imagination, we give him the mythology of the world by which humans have explained natural laws. Language skills are developed through written expression of this work, and math and geometry come alive as tools to measure these discoveries.

Children can keep their own lab manuals or individual records of the work and discoveries in this area. The scientific method of recording experiments follows a traditional format: selecting an experiment, gathering materials, following the steps to test the hypothesis, observing, and recording the results.

Timelines are used in all areas of the elementary curriculum. For an interesting timeline, make a long strip of cloth or paper, marking the years in the billions, millions, thousands — like the markings on a ruler — from the beginning of earth's creation to the present. Next figure out for how long there have been plants and animals and color this part of the timeline one color. Then mark, with another color, the length of time humans have been here. This is a powerful image for children and adults. Timelines can be made for all different subjects, tracing the history of the natural world, the development of the mapping of the earth, the discovery of elements, and so forth. The arts play a large part of every area of the elementary studies. Models, plays enacting historical dramas such as the measurement of the earth, songs, artwork–there is no end to the possibilities.

BIOLOGY, LIFE SCIENCES

Every Montessori class is unique. This timeline of wine production is from a school in Rome, Italy, where growing grapes and making wine has always been a very important part of the culture.

How often is the soul of man, especially that of the child, deprived because one does not put him in contact with nature. There is no description, no image in any book, that is capable of replacing the sight of real trees, and all the life to be found around them, in a real forest. Something emanates from those trees which speaks to the soul, something no book, no museum is capable of giving. The wood reveals that it is not only the trees that exist, but a whole, interrelated collection of lives. And this earth, this climate, this cosmic power is necessary for the development of all these lives. The myriad lives around the trees, the majesty, the variety, are things one must hunt for, and which no one can bring into the school.

—**Maria Montessori**

In the 6-12 class the study of biology has three main focuses:

1) Experiments and observation of plants and animals to discover the amazing variety and needs of plants and animals

2) Evolution of plants and animals throughout time

3) Classification of plants and animals

At the beginning of each year the teacher inspires children to carry out research in these areas by telling stories, and presenting beautiful books, posters, charts, and timelines, that excite the imagination and make children want to know more. Then each child begins a personal journey of discovery, joining others for research projects and presentations. Every year is unpredictable, not even the teacher knowing what will be covered, as the rule is to "follow the child."

Experiments and observations help the child discover first hand just how plants and animals live, to find out how their needs are met, and to discover the amazing variety of life forms. Children become aware of the world in a new way, discovering the tiny plants in the cracks of pavements — growing wherever they can find a little light, moisture, and nourishment. This close-hand experience makes children appreciative and protective of all of life.

Experiments and observation lead to discoveries that help the child travel, through his tremendous imagination, back through time to the very beginning of life, to discover the miracle of variety and the transformation of plants and animals through time. The children will go to the original sources for information, for example, the writings of Charles Darwin that are very interesting. Thus they begin to learn the difference between getting information second-hand, interpreted by someone, and the original, or primary, source.

The discovery of the multitude of kinds of plants and animals, and the fact that each language has a different name for each kind, helps children understand why there must be a system of sorting and naming them—this is biological classification. Children are naturally curious about why plants and animals have been classified and named as they have been, and how the systems of classification change as we learn more about biology. This kind of intellectual inquiry is valid in all areas and particularly leads to curiosity about the connection between biology, logic, math, and language, history, and Latin. When subjects are presented in a way that connects all areas of study, when it is the child who comes up with the questions, and when the child is allowed to follow his interest, facts become part of his long-term memory instead of just being memorized, tested on, and forgotten. Biology can become a lifelong interest for this child.

The child from birth on is constantly learning his body, from the way he was handled as an infant, from how he learns to care for and feed himself, even the way those around him respect and treat their own bodies and others. A natural and healthy attitude develops about bodies and sex if these topics are part of the daily conversation at home and at school. Otherwise a child is put into the position of learning about these things from the media or from other questionable sources. Caring for our bodies and learning to respect the bodies of other people, sex, love, relationships, families — what could be more important information for us to pass on correctly to our children during these very curious years from age six to twelve, and beyond.

THE HUMANITIES, SOCIAL SCIENCES

*In this classroom in Canada, making model
pyramids brings the study of Egypt, and other
civilizations of the past, to life.*

*Today those things that occupy us in the field of
education are the interests of humanity at large and
of civilization. Before such great forces we can
recognize only one country — the entire world.*
— **Maria Montessori**

The history of a people cannot be separated from the
influences, limits, support, of the environment in which
it develops, and the leadership of its great men and
women. In the beginning of each year the children are
introduced to the study of humankind with stories,
books, maps, posters, timelines and other research
inspirations. Throughout the six years in the elementary

class, the child moves from the general to the specific in the following way:

Age 6-8: The emphasis at this age in the 6-12 class is on prehistoric life, and plants and animals. He learns how plants and animals developed based on their environment and the changing climate of the Earth. He studies the amazing variety of species that leads naturally into the study of classification—and the study of botany and zoology

Age 8-10: The emphasis is on early civilizations, from tribal cultures and ancient civilizations to the development of modern cities. The study includes exploration of the causes and results of migrations and how this is connected to the development of language and cultures, and the sciences.

Age 10-12: The emphasis is on the child's national and state history. The foundation has been laid in the first four years of the 6-12 class and this makes the study of one's own continent, country, state, county, city, one's own culture, make sense. Of course all of these studies are going on at the same time and the child is free to follow his interests, no matter what the age. It is reinforced by the very important element of the Montessori class, that is that children teach each other, and they go to each other for help. As I have said, the 6-year-old is exposed to the work of the 11-year-old, and the older child improves and increases her own knowledge because of the act of teaching someone else.

Those who do not remember the past are condemned to relive it.
— George Santayana, philosopher, Harvard University

History is essentially a record of how humans fulfilled their physical, mental, and spiritual needs. These can be classified as follows: Physical needs: food, clothing, shelter, transportation, and defense; Mental tendencies: work, exploration, creation, communication, play; Spiritual needs: self-respect or self love, love of others, creative love and the love of God, or contact with something outside of oneself.

These subjects are also experienced subjectively in the classroom. For example, as the child learns about how different people obtain food, he learns to grow and prepare food. As he learns about clothing he may learn to knit or to make clothing or costumes. He studies the arts of other cultures while developing his own musical and other artistic talents. And while studying the ethics and religions of other cultures he is exploring his own relationship with friends, family, and God. This creates not only new abilities, but also an empathy with members of other cultures in the present and the past.

The history of his own country is introduced after the child has learned about the creation of the solar system, the earth, the coming of plants and animals, his study of local history begins with the first presence of humans in his own country. As an example, American history begins with the study of those who first arrived on this continent, not the immigration of Europeans. It is the story of the Native Americans and the people from all over the world who have settled here. An excellent way to make this point is to take a long role of adding machine paper and put the dates from, say 20,000 BC (or whenever humans arrived in North America according to the most recent archaeological findings) to the present. Then make little cards with pictures and dates to show the relationship of events in time. Some suggestions are "crossing the Bering Straits," "Height of Aztec civilization" (and as many other Native American events as the parent or teacher and the children can find) "Columbus arrives", "the ipod was invented" and so forth. Laying the cards gives an impression or overview of American history. Use timelines for any subject.

The first biographies children study are their parents and grandparents, their friends, and their teachers — and this begins early. As teenagers, our children will operate on information about relationships, marriage, parenting, teaching, working, honesty, love, and so on, that they learned from living with us, their parents, grandparents, teachers! As our children go on to learn about the great men and women of the past it is important that we remind them that these people all started out as children just as they are now — and that the potential to be great and to contribute to the world is in all of us. Here is a quote that expresses this idea beautifully:

> *Each second we live is a new and unique*
> *moment in the universe — a moment that was never*

before and will never be again. What we teach our
children in school is 2+2=4 and Paris is the capital of
France. When will we teach them what they are?
What we should say to them is: Do you know what
you are? You are a marvel! You are unique! In all
the world there is no other child exactly like you! In
the millions of years that have passed, there has
never been a child exactly like you. Look at your
body, what a wonder it is! Your legs, your arms,
your cunning fingers, and the way you move! You
may be a Shakespeare, a Michelangelo, a Beethoven .
. . you have the capacity for anything. Yes, you are a
marvel. And when you grow up, can you then harm
another who is like you a marvel?
                        — Pablo Casals, Cellist

The study of history, biography, and geography in
the Montessori elementary class is different each year
depending on the curiosity and research of each group of
students. There are basic lessons that the teacher gives at
the beginning of the year to present an overview and an
outline for research. But one never knows where the
children will take it, where the individual interests will
lead. This is thrilling for the teacher and the children
alike, and the children never forget what they learn.

THE ARTS

*Art expresses all of the work in
the elementary class, as is demonstrated
by this Thai student's book about the
evolution of life on Earth.*

*Imagination does not become great until a
person, given the courage and strength, uses it to
create. If this does not occur, the imagination
addresses itself only to a spirit wandering in
emptiness.*

— **Maria Montessori**

All of the academic work in the elementary class is
connected with, and expressed by means of the arts:
plays, as unique as the acting out the process of
photosynthesis (the children write the plays based on
their interests), maps of the population of the world, a
quilt made with squares of leaf shapes, a series of
beautiful watercolors demonstrating the principles of

104

geometry — there is no limit to the creativity. Just as in all areas, the teacher is in charge of teaching the use of the tools, and the students of designing and executing the work.

When we look at the curricula of the past, the Greeks and the Tibetans for example, we see that music and dance, and the arts in general, were an important part of the classical education. The arts were considered "the basics," perhaps because they had discovered that purely academic learning was boring and unhealthy. When information is processed in some active, musical, or artistic way — graphs, posters, drawings, creating maps, songs, plays, and so forth, the knowledge becomes permanent and it strengthens the creative part of the brain. When a student becomes interested in a particular topic, the adult's role is to supply what is needed, and then respect the child's ideas and expression. Studying the creations of other cultures, experiencing their dances and music, studying the reasons why different architectural forms developed, and clothing or language, gives a child an understanding of the universality of human needs and expression.

LANGUAGE

Once an "explosion" into reading begins, all we can do is help find the right books and get out of the way!

A love of reading comes about quite naturally for a child who grows up hearing others tell stories, seeing them read for pleasure, and being read to. Seeing others writing notes, grocery lists, "thank you" notes, and recording personal experiences and thoughts, will make a child want to do the same. Telling stories, and then writing stories illustrated with drawings, can begin at a very early age. A nightly ritual of family reading (instead of watching TV) is a good way to make sure that there is time for all the great literature and poetry that you might want to read to your child. In our family we as parents have filled in many a gap in our own literary and factual knowledge by reading to our children.

Poetry brings more important elements into the child's language; there is a great increase in vocabulary when one delves into poetry. Even in the simplest forms words are used that are not common in prose. The music of poetry gives greater pleasure and facilitates memorization. Our favorite kinds of poetry are those that can be read aloud, like a Greek chorus, or which tell long stories, such as the Pied Piper.

It sometimes happens, however, that a child becomes disinterested in reading on his own because he is afraid this nightly ritual will come to an end. To prevent this we can assure the child that we will continue to read as long as he desires. In our home we read to our children even during their teenage years, and even when they returned home on a college vacation, to the delight of all.

Learning to read well can take years. During this time the child benefits immensely from being read to — from great literature and non-fiction. This is how he learns correct pronunciation of new words that increase his vocabulary, and teaches himself how to read with correct intonation and expression. But most of all he needs, and perhaps never outgrows the need for, the love and the closeness, the personal attention from parents, a friend or a teacher, that comes with curling up with a book, picturing the magic scenes in his head with his eyes closed as he listens, and listens.

The child over seven is intensely interested in morals and heroes. Mythology provides a wealth of material for this exploration, and inspires discussion that will encompass behavior in everyday life, in the family, the class, and society.

If a child learns to read in a motor-sensorial way, by means of sandpaper letters and movable alphabets, with no pressure she may learn before the age of five or six, but it is quite natural for a child not to show an interest until later. The most important thing is that learning be a relaxed and enjoyable experience.

When a child first begins to read independently, we never ask him to read aloud. To process the decoding of a word, while at the same time saying aloud the previous word aloud, is a very complex operation and can cause a lot of stress when a child is asked to carry out both processes at the same time when first beginning. This is certainly not an enjoyable and stress-free way to begin. Instead we give beginning readers, vocabulary cards, labels to match with the cards, and vocabulary books to help build up a large vocabulary with no stress. The best first books are written about the child's environment, about the real world—history, sciences, etc. And it is important that the child had been introduced to most of the ideas and words verbally before he is asked to read them. Also there are sometimes abridged classics that can be read to the child, and then be among the first books he will read, and this can lead to an interest in great literature.

> *I hear and I forget. I see and I remember.*
> *I write and I understand.* **— Chinese Proverb**

A child who has had an active physical and mental life, using his hands in more and more refined activities such as running, hopping, balancing while walking on a thin line, spooning, pouring, cooking, sewing, drawing, digging, playing with clay, will usually find writing easier than children who have been more passive in their learning.

When the child first begins to write we do not make corrections with either grammar or spelling. We "teach by teaching, not by correcting." Instead we teach all the necessary skills through activities that are completely unrelated to the creative writing effort, as indirect preparation. We do not give the traditional spelling word lists of words that will never be in the child's writing vocabulary. There are really three different kinds of vocabulary. The first is the one we use in our everyday talking. The second is the one we use in our every day writing. The third is the one that we use in reading. All three are constantly expanding, but it is the second that we need to focus in helping the child with learning to spell. The following is a suggestion for teaching the spelling of words one will be most likely to use in writing.

A child's personal spelling dictionary: Most of the words in the spelling lists usually given to children to learn are seldom really used. In Montessori classes the child constructs his "spelling dictionary" of words that are a part of his individual writing vocabulary. For this you can use a simple address book, preferably one without any writing in it, just the alphabetized tabs. But since such books are not much used these days it is better to make one by cutting tabs into the pages of a small notebook, or buying alphabetized tabs to fasten to the pages. Whenever a child comes to you for the spelling of a word, or if he asks you to check the words he has written and you find some misspelled, write these words — beautifully of course because you are the model for writing — in his spelling dictionary, words beginning with 'a' in the 'a' section and so forth. But it is not enough that these words be identified and beautifully recorded by the adult. The purpose is that they are learned. This is done by looking in the personal dictionary when the word is needed, and by having little tests, and some children learn best by writing these words multiple times. The next time he wants a particular word for his own fiction or non-fiction writing, he will be able to find it in his own book.

To learn to spell the words in one's personal spelling dictionary in class the children can have spelling tests among themselves to learn their own "writing" vocabulary. I suggest beginning these spelling tests when there are only 2-3 words in the dictionary, then regularly from then on as the list becomes larger. This shows the child, with each test, that he has indeed learned to spell some of his favorite words. He will discover that there are not so many words one really needs to learn in order to express oneself. This will gradually give the child confidence to learn and to use more and more words — they will have been collected in his own book. I find that this inspires confidence in spelling, makes writing fun, and challenges some children to start to use a continually growing writing vocabulary, which can sometimes grow by leaps and bounds.

Beautiful writing has been a lost art in our country for many years but it is experiencing a resurgence. Children feel very good about themselves and tend to write far more when they have been taught beautiful handwriting. Giving a child a new alphabet and a different kind of writing utensil often does wonders to inspire writing. The Italic script is very beautiful and a link between cursive and print. I have seen a child's cursive writing improve dramatically as he casually worked through a set of Italic workbooks over a period of months.

Brain research today helps us understand the process of learning, of making a new skill a habit. It is important to understand this when helping a child learn to write. The cortex is used in learning to write. The formation of each letter activates a specific set of neurons in the brain. As the formation of a letter is repeated over and over gradually it is "learned," and the neurons needed to form letters are now those in the lower part of the brain, the habit area controlling activities that have become automatic. At this point the neurons in the brain that were previously activated in the cortex shrink and prepare for new challenges, new skills to be learned.

Think about this. Each time a child writes a letter badly, repeating it over and over, the ugly way of writing this letter become more and more "learned" and eventually is related to the lower part of the brain. It will be very difficult for him to ever write that letter beautifully.

When I learned this I understood why my teacher Margaret Stephenson said to never ask a child to write anything that he cannot write beautifully. And do not criticize ugly writing because after all it is the adult that allowed ugly writing to develop. Instead she suggested that at this time, the beginning of the 6-12 stage of development, we introduce a new script. If the child had learned print before this, introduce cursive. If he has learned cursive, introduce italics. This helps him slow down and work carefully on the formation of letters. She suggested that we introduce colored inks to make the process even more carefully with the results being even more beautiful. I followed her advice, even giving beautifully written short poems for the child to copy, and to decorate the margins with these same colored inks.

One day an 8-year old who had been asked to write every day in a journal in his previous school, asked me quietly if I would help him learned to write "better." He was very interesting to talk to, and had original ideas on every subject, and loved to share them. But he could only do this verbally because he said he hated to write. I gave him a lined piece of paper and at the beginning of the first line wrote, as slowly and beautifully as I possible, a cursive letter. I asked him to fill the line with that letter as slowly has I had done. When he was finished together we studied each letter he had written, discussing each in detail. "Had it touched the base line? Had it reached the top line? What do we think of the slope? And the width of the loops?" Then I asked him to circle the letter that he decided was closest to the model. After several letters I asked if he would like to write some words using these letters, or a sentence. I should not have done that; it was too early. His face fell and he said, "I can't and I hate to write *ugly*!" He was a perfect example of someone who had, because he was required to write when he had not been taught to write beautifully, learned well how to write badly, and he now had to completely rewire parts of his brain. Not an easy task.

Sometimes it is said that beautiful writing is no longer necessary because our children will be using computers. But writing is far more than just practical, and I hope we are leaning that being in front of a computer screen is not necessarily the best place to spend one's time. Just as it has been shown that people who depend on a calculator for all of their math never learn how to estimate, and are at a loss when they have to use their own brain for math, writing is a skill that has more than just practical applications. "Thank you" notes should be a regular part of a child's life from as early as possible, and they should always be hand-written. Condolence notes the same. Writing is an expression of who we are, and the beautiful handwriting is good for a child's self-image and his brain. Children who learn to write with a script that they are proud of are far more likely to write in general than those who find is frustrating. I hope I have convinced you to help your child learn to write as well as he possibly can, and to enjoy your own handwriting.

As the child is learning about the history of humans on earth, about the history of civilizations, in the geography and history areas, it is quite natural that this interest flows into the study of languages. Through stories, pictures and beautiful carefully chosen books, we enable the child to begin to understand:

1) The path traced by language, the growth, and development of language — through, colonization, commerce, and war.

2) How humans have given a name to everything found or made and how this process continues

3) How language constantly changes and why

4) How language expresses the creative force of humanity

At this age children in many ways are repeating the history of humans on earth. They want to cook, sew, garden, and begin to learn all of the skills of adults. Children and adults alike find it fascinating to trace the development of the language, to realize that in the past only a few people, sometimes only priests, knew how to read and write. They find the connection between the migrations and other contacts between groups of people and the many different languages on earth. And they are amazed the even today there are millions of children all over the world who cannot read and write and because of this are severely limited in what choices they will have in their lives. This makes children appreciate their own good fortune in being able to learn.

Etymology, the origin and historical development of words, is fascinating to children at this age. It is a fine basis for learning to spell, and contributes to understanding the history of cultures. When our children were growing up we always kept a very large dictionary always available on a special table in the living room. It was not allowed to place anything else upon the table so that the dictionary was always easily opened and usable. We often looked up the etymology of words even more often than the definitions. If you are planning to purchase a dictionary I recommend that you make sure that the origin of words is included along with the pronunciation and definition.

Children often take names of people and places for granted, assuming that they existed from the beginning of time. Imagine the amount of history and geography one can learn from stories of how people and places were named. Studying the history of names, first names and last names, is a wonderful way to interest children in language and history. Most of us have completely lost touch with the history of our families for more than two or three generations, and have no idea how and why we are named what we are. This information can inspire a neverending study of language. Every year I took my 6-12 school children to a local cemetery. I just showed them a few gravestones, and each group became interested in a different aspect of this experience. Some wanted to make a list of the countries and languages represented. Others wanted to make a timeline of the very earliest date to the present. One child wanted to figure out the age of every single person when he died, and others to make rubbings with paper and crayon of some of the raised pictures of letters. This is a perfect example of how children quite naturally move from one academic area of study to another from their own curiosity.

As adults we may have unpleasant memories of learning grammar. Usually these studies were considered very difficult and taught at a period of life when we were not really interested in language. It works best to follow the child's interest and this is the time of life when children are very interested in the progress of civilization, including language — including the structure of their own language.

Many great educators and philosophers have stated that there is nothing that cannot be taught if the student and the subject matter are well understood and creatively put in touch with each other. We try to make everything interesting, so that it will be enjoyed and retained.

INVENTION, GEOMETRY, AND MATH

In this country school in Thailand students begin to understand mechanics and physics as they learn to care for the school lawn mower.

Invention, geometry, and math are languages used to explore, manipulate, create, and measure real objects in a real world. At this age children continue to enjoy exploring math and geometry concepts if they are related to real life, and if they are presented with materials that can be handled, manipulated, used to create. We must keep sight of this fact when teaching children. We give manipulative materials in all areas of math and leave it to each child to decide when she is ready to move on, to work without materials—in the abstract—on paper with pencil. This abstract work is a higher mental level of work, which comes naturally after the child has learned to picture the object being measured or related to other objects in her mind.

In the 6-12 class stories are told and experiments carried out that illustrate how humans used their imaginations in the past, and how they are using them today, to solve problems and come up with great inventions—the use of fire, measuring the earth, compasses, the wheel, boats, and many others. They see how inventions, geometry, and math came about as the result of human progress, to meet specific needs, and how language is a reflection of these things. Geometry, for example, arose from the practical need to reestablish planting boundaries after the annual flooding of the Nile in Egypt. And the word comes from Ancient Greek (ge, "earth, land, country") + (metreo, "to measure, to count").

Children of this age love to reach back into history with their imaginations and reconstruct these needs and solutions and the creation of systems of learning. The Hindus introduced the use of "0." Let the children try to do math without it and see what happens! Where did algebra, calculus, trigonometry come from? Children want to know the answers to these questions. The adult does not have to have the answers; it is more important to tell children when we don't know, and help them learn to find the answers for themselves.

Children are inspired by these stories, and by examples and pictures, to find out more. Children come to realize that mathematics has evolved and is still evolving from a practical need. Math, graphing, fractions, all become logical tools for recording and measuring, and algebra a short cut for recording.

In solving problems, we encourage children to make up their own story and number problems — especially story problems related to their lives and the subjects they are studying — for themselves and for their friends. This helps a child come to a very practical and clear understanding of geometry and math. Children enjoy making up problems for each other, and examples that stump their teachers. This process of math concepts makes them stick in the mind. With higher math, geometry, and algebra, we give many practical examples and help the children come up with their own formulae after much experience. For example, if a child measures all of the rectangles in the room — tables, windows, books, etc. for figuring surface area, he will easily create, and even better understand, the formula "A=lw."

For each grade level, from 1st through 6th, the children are shown the state requirements of math, just as any other subject. Then they learn to plan and schedule their work. It is left to each child to decide the best system and schedule, through trial and error, and with adult help, depending on learning styles, and interests. This teaches the math of planning, scheduling, allotting sufficient time, and it teaches responsibility. When children are given this solid, material foundation, and see the relationship of geometry and math to the real world, it makes it easier for them, in later years, to spend long periods of time working on paper. This is because they know that these steps are just that—steps that will take them to a new level of understanding in the exciting world of math and science.

PART THREE, AGE 0-24

STAGES OF DEVELOPMENT

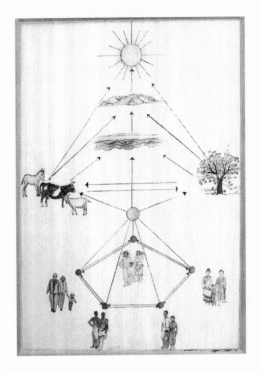

*An example of the "Cosmic Task" chart
showing interrelationship and inspiring each
child to find his place in the Cosmos.*

One of the most valuable of Dr. Montessori's ideas, in meeting the needs of children, is called the "Stages of Development." The child's needs are continually changing as he grows, and in order to have all needs met for optimum development, the environment must also change. This is sometimes explained by examples of nature. A seed, for example, in order to sprout, needs to be in the dark. As it sprouts and turns into a plant it needs warmth, light, water, and nutrients if it is to thrive. When a corn plant is out in the field it needs a steady supply of wind to strengthen the stem so it does not just fall over under the weight of ears of corn as they develop. Another example is the frog. It needs a specific temperature of water for the eggs to grow in a pond, then water and food as it grows as a tadpole with a tail and gills, and then air as it becomes a creature that will live on land and breathe by means of lungs. We humans cannot tell a plant or an amphibian at what stage it needs what. We can only provide the environment and trust that the plant and amphibian has the information to guide it in taking what it needs from the environment to support its optimum development. It is similar with humans. It is similar with our children.

When the environment, including the adults, give children from conception all they need, physically, emotionally, even the very young will be able to use their own internal wisdom to fulfill their needs and develop their fullest potential. Dr. Montessori divided these stages roughly as follows:

0-6, the beginning of childhood

6-12, the completion of childhood

12-18, the beginning of adulthood

18-24, the completion of becoming an adult

Following are some examples of these stages.

Age 0-6, The Absorbent Mind

This period of life is by far the most dynamic. Imagine a being who at birth has no physical abilities except to nurse, to look around, to listen, and to cry. Within the first year he learns to turn over, crawl, to pull up, to stand, to walk, to use his hands intentionally, to make his needs known verbally, to communicate. All this occurs in just 12 months.

And before age six a child can learn to dance and sing, to speak perfectly as many languages as he is exposed to, to use perfect grammar, to use thousands of words, to care for others, to use his mind and body in ways that we adults find amazing if we stop and think about it. No stage in life can begin to compare with what is accomplished at this time. In the first six years of life children literally absorb the world around them with no effort on their part, the good, and the bad. We can never be too kind, polite, respectful, to be their role models. When others are caring them for we must have the highest standard of expectation for these vitally influential adults.

The 3-6 Montessori school environment is called a *casa dei bambini*, or house of children because it is very different from the traditional school. It really is more like a house. To imagine the difference think of how you act when welcoming friends into your own inviting, comfortable, enjoyable home. Would you have everyone, all of your guests in your home, sit still on a line and put their hands in their lap and close their mouths? Or would you have specially prepared interesting activities, perhaps some food, and welcome each person with a personal greeting, inviting her to make herself at home? Would you line up chairs and tables, labeling where your guests were to sit? Or would you arrange the home with paintings, comfortable chairs, plants, and soft music? If a guest in your home appeared at loose ends would you tell him to get to work, or would you have a private conversation with him and offer some interesting activity? When your guests were all settled in and having a lovely time would you interrupt them and tell them to come and sit in a circle because what you have to show them is more important than anything they might be doing?

From age 0-6 children are invited, but never required, to carry out certain tasks. There are only two rules in a 3-6 class.

1) We (including adults as well as children) don't interrupt someone who is concentrating.

2) One can work with any material whose purpose one understands — having learned it from the teacher or from another child.

The adult observes carefully to meet the child's physical, mental, and emotional needs. Once a child has been attracted to an activity, and has begun to concentrate, the adult respects this choice and concentration and does not interrupt. Children are taught, through fun role-playing lessons such as the game of introductions that requires us to look into the other person's face, grasp their right hand firmly, and say, "How you do?" (Or whatever is appropriate in the child's culture).

Children want to learn how to move gracefully and carefully. An example in the classroom is known as "walking on the line." Rather than constantly reminding a child not to run inside, a line is painted or sometimes taped on the floor and the child is shown how to walk, at first just staying on the line, then with toe touching heel, and then with further challenges such as with a small pillow on his head, walking so carefully that it does not fall off. Or carrying a soup bowl of water, or a bell, the challenge being walking so steadily that it does not ring.

Aside from these grace and courtesy lessons, at this age we give the child, who is voraciously devouring experiences, the basic elements of all future studies — motor-sensorial experience that proved keys to later study in biology, art, geography, geometry, math, music, and language.

Age 6-12

This is a very stable and a more intellectual age. At this period, other than a gradual increase in size, one does not see the great changes that occur from birth to six years, and from 12-15. For that reason there can be an emphasis on practical and academic work. The 6-12 child is interested in the ways in which society functions, how it came into being. He wants to participate in real work, and to explore the past and the farthest reaches of the universe with the imagination, to see and understand the universe and the development of humanity. This child can make incredible advances in intellectual work as he goes out into society and learns to function independently, in and outside school.

THE YOUNG ADULT, AGE 12-18

The skills of caring for the environment, such as cleaning the pond at this school in Thailand, will always be valuable.

The focus continues to be on the needs and tendencies of the young person, *not* just on the academic requirements of today. The world is changing far too rapidly for us to assume that we know what these academic requirements are, or to know what children will need to have learned in even ten years from now. But we do know that he will need to know how to be happy, to be kind, to make intelligent choices, to solve problems, to help each other, and to enjoy doing a good job in all kinds of work. More information on this period of life follows.

A child who had experienced independence — going to the grocery store on his own, finding books in a public library, interacting with people outside the school and family — by the end of the stable age of six to twelve — will have a better chance of experiencing a happy transition from adolescence to adult life: going to college, moving out into the adult world, earning a living, and perhaps taking care of a spouse and children.

This third period of development can be divided into 12-15 and 15-18 because the needs are different. In the first three years of the developmental stage there is again, as in the first period from 0-6, tremendous growth, and new hormones create great changes. This child needs more sleep and less stress. Some schools have become aware of the need for more sleep and are even beginning the school day later. Dr. Montessori recommended a situation where children would live close to nature, eat fresh farm products, and carry on practical work related to supplying food, shelter, transportation, and running a business. Intellectual subjects are still taught, following the child's interests, but without the pressure of the traditional school at this age.

When a child enters adolescence he/she becomes physically capable of becoming a parent and takes an interest in this part of growing up. It is quite common for Montessori teachers of children from 12-15 to take the 0-3 training for two reasons. First it is helpful because there are similarities in the children in the 0-3 stage of life, and the 12-15, the rapid growth, etc. And because this is the perfect time for young people to learn about pregnancy, birth, parenting, and child development.

Years ago I was teaching adolescents in a Montessori school on a Caribbean island. A very bright 13-year-old boy was having trouble concentrating on math and other purely intellectual subjects, so I watched carefully to discover his real abilities and interests, which were: house, job, music, and parenting. In our class the children designed and developed long-term research projects and presentations. This boy was behind in academic areas so I helped him weave his interests into projects that would utilize skills that he needed to practice. He spent hours planning his dream house, complete with indoor swimming pool and skateboard area. In doing this he researched houses of various cultures and used plenty of math, graphing, and geometry in constructing the house plans. He did a feasibility study for beginning a skateboard construction-and-repair business–rents, prices of equipment, market value of skateboards and labor costs. As his confidence grew he branched out into other academic areas. Then he became interested in literature, and began to study piano, recorder, and guitar in class using classical and folk instruction books and asking for help when he needed it. This study of music provided the greatest practice in self-discipline as he scheduled daily practice and was still able to complete his other work. It seemed to help him express the changing

129

emotions that otherwise would have no constructive outlet. And the personal and social rewards were immediate.

But along with this classroom success it was this boy's interest in parenting that was most intriguing to observe. Here was this tall, gangly, adolescent boy, leading the group on the softball field, but if he heard a cry or yell of one of the children in the 3-6 class at the other end of the campus, he immediately put down the bat and ran to see what was the matter. There was one three-year-old in particular, Paloma, who seemed to have captured his fathering heart. They had only just met at the Montessori school, but he could single out her voice from all others, from quite a distance, and would always go to her aid. More than anything else, at this time when intellectual skills had been low it was his being needed as a protector by the young gave him a feeling of worth.

As I have worked in pre-industrial cultures such as Bhutan, I have seen children go through this period of life, from 12-18, with none of the difficulties we come to believe are universal. There are no special labels such as pre-teen, or teenagers. People just gradually become adults, taking on responsibilities as they become more and more capable. It reminds me of this quote:

> *Adolescence is an arbitrary, contrived category.*
> *In past eras children were children until the early*
> *teens wherein, through some rite of passage, they*
> *were ushered into and took their place in adult*

society. Today there is no economic place for young
adults and no rites of passage. We have, instead,
created a holding stage that keeps young people in
limbo, into which children enter earlier and adults
stay longer year-by-year.
— **Joseph Chilton Pearce,** *Evolution's End*

From age fifteen to eighteen, when the rapid physical and emotional growth of adolescence is slowing, a more rigorous intellectual schedule works, combined with social work and apprenticeships can be managed. There are many Montessori schools for children in the middle and high school years in the USA today that try to follow the directive of Dr. Montessori:

The need that is so keenly felt for a reform of
secondary schools concerns not only an educational,
but also a human and social problem. Schools, as
they are today, are adapted neither to the needs of
adolescents nor to the times in which we live. Society
has not only developed into a state of utmost
complication and extreme contrasts, but it has now
come to a crisis in which the peace of the world and
civilization itself are threatened.... More than to
anything else it is due to the fact that the
development of man himself has not kept pace with
that of his external environment.

But above all it is the education of adolescents
that is important, because adolescence is the time
when the child enters on the state of manhood and
becomes a member of society. If puberty is on the

physical side a transition from an infantile to an adult state, there is also, on the psychological side, a transition from the child to the adult who has to live in society. These two needs of the adolescent: for protection during the time of the difficult physical transition, and for an understanding of the society which he is about to enter to play his part as a man, give rise to two problems that are of equal importance concerning education at this age.

The world is partly in a state of disintegration and partly in a state of reconstruction.... It is necessary that the human personality should be prepared for the unforeseen, not only for the conditions that can be anticipated by prudence and foresight...he must be strengthened in his principles by moral training and he must also have practical ability in order to face the difficulties of life. Men with hands and no head, and men with head and no hands are equally out of place in the modern community.

Education should not limit itself to seeking new methods for a mostly arid transmission of knowledge: its aim must be to give the necessary aid to human development. This world, marvelous in its power, needs a 'new man'. It is therefore the life of man and his values that must be considered. If 'the formation of man' becomes the basis of education, then the coordination of all schools from infancy to maturity, from nursery to university, arises as a first necessity.
— **Maria Montessori**

In Montessori 6-12 classes children learn how to balance and schedule their time, to set work goals and to accomplish them, and often the skills in budgeting and handling money. In an *Erdkinder*, or farm school, for ages 12 –15, children will have had even more experience in handling money as they sometimes take care of gardens and sell the produce, or become involved with other real economic projects. If they have this experience by high school they will be more prepared for the economic responsibilities of adulthood, even being able to participate in planning the budget of the home.

One of the most important lessons is the realization of just how much time and work is involved in earning money. There are few jobs for teenagers, and those that pay a salary are usually not educational. A better place to learn might be an unpaid apprenticeship. However it is time-consuming for most professionals to take the time to teach an untrained person. Young people should be aware of this and look for what they can offer or learn, instead of what they can get in the way of salary. Apprenticeships are not paid positions, but they can be extremely beneficial to the students, and sometimes open up important job possibilities in the future.

When this is not possible we can help a young person look for other ways to be helpful on a volunteer basis. But I would stress that the reason behind volunteer work should not be "to look good on one's college application" but instead to learn about the value of work, to explore non-academic skills in interests and improve them, and most of all to experience how good it feels, and how important it is, to help others.

It is important that young people who are fortunate enough to earn money for some of their work get into the habit of using their earnings for necessities of life such as food and transportation, not just for entertainment and purchasing unnecessary "toys." This will help them learn the real value of money, the real connection between work and providing for one's needs. Here is an article published years ago but still valid today, and shared in many Montessori schools:

> By the '80's, three out of four high-school seniors were working an average of 18 hours a week and often taking home more than $200 a month. But their jobs, often in fast-food chains, were rarely challenging and earnings were immediately spent on cars, clothing, stereos, and other artifacts of the adolescent good life. Indeed, researchers at the University of Michigan find that less than 11 percent of high-school seniors save all or most of their earnings for college or other long-range purposes. In short, teenage employment has only intensified the adolescent drive for immediate gratification. Instead of learning how to delay desires, students are indulging in what University of Michigan researcher Jerome Bachman calls "premature affluence." The problem, says Bachman, is that these adolescents tend to get accustomed to an unrealistic level of discretionary income which is

impossible to maintain at college, unless they have extravagant parents. "And if they don't go to school," he observes, "they will have to continue to live at home if they hope to keep up their personal spending habits."

—**Kenneth Woodward**, *Newsweek*,
"Young Beyond their Years"(1990)

The Adult, Age 18-24

Very young students in this boarding school in Nepal learn to do real work and by high school are sterilizing tools and keeping records for the annual dental clinic run by volunteer USA dentists.

Some educators recommend a year off between high school and university to give young people a chance to experience real life and its effort and responsibilities, and to learn who they are and where their interests lie. Both of our daughters had that experience just after high school. Each had moved into an apartment within a few blocks of our very small home in California. I remember the end of the first week of our first daughter's experience when she came to me and said, "I can't believe how much time it takes to go to work, do the laundry, buy food and clean. It takes all my time when I am not at work. I don't know how you do it!" Ahhh, she was starting to learn.

Here are two favorite relevant quotes:

It is not enough to teach a man a specialty. Through it he may become a kind of useful machine but not a harmoniously developed personality. It is essential that the student acquire an understanding of and a lively feeling for values. He must acquire a vivid sense of the beautiful and the morally good. Otherwise he – with his specialized knowledge – more closely resembles a well-trained dog than a harmoniously developed person. He must learn to understand the motives of human beings, their illusions, and their sufferings in order to acquire a proper relationship to individual fellow men and to the community.

These precious things are conveyed to the younger generation through personal contact with those who teach, not – or at least not in the main – through textbooks. It is this that primarily constitutes and preserves culture. This is what I have in mind when I recommend the 'humanities' as important, not just dry specialized knowledge in the fields of history and philosophy.

Overemphasis on the competitive system and premature specialization on the ground of immediate usefulness kill the spirit on which all cultural life depends, specialized knowledge included. It is also vital to a valuable education that independent critical thinking be developed in the young human beings, a development that is greatly jeopardized by

*overburdening him with too much and with too
varied subjects (point system). Overburdening
necessarily leads to superficiality. Teaching should
be such that what is offered is perceived as a valuable
gift and not as a hard duty.*

— Albert Einstein, "Education for Independent
Thought," (New York Times, 1952)

*And how far, we may ask, does it take one to
hold a degree these days? (Written in 1949) Can one
be sure of even earning a living? And how do we
explain this lack of confidence? The reason is that
these young men have spent years in listening to
words and listening does not make a man. Only
practical work and experience lead the young to
maturity. My vision of the future is no longer of
people taking exams and proceeding on that
certification from the secondary school to the
university, but of individuals passing from one stage
of independence to a higher, by means of their own
activity, through their own effort of will, which
constitutes the inner evolution of the individual.*

— Maria Montessori

For Everything There is a Season. It is not good for
children to be pushed into stages that they are not ready
for. But neither is it good for us to hold children back
when they are ready to move on. At any age, an
unnecessary aid is really a hindrance to development.
Dr. Montessori speaks for the child when she says, of the
child's desire: "Please help me to do it myself!"

PART FOUR
PARENTS AND TEACHERS

PREPARING A LEARNING ENVIRONMENT

Nature is a vital part of the "learning environment." Here the author is showing a sunflower seastar (Pycnopodia helianthoides) to her eldest grandchild.

Constant preparation and adaptation of the environment to the ever-changing needs and tendencies of growing children is essential in the Montessori method of raising and educating children. The first consideration is physical safety, and then the proper support for free movement, exploration, making choices, concentrating, creating, completing cycles — all of which contribute to the optimum development of the child. Natural materials are used instead of plastic, and attention is paid to simplicity, muted colors, plants, and beauty, all contributing to the mental and physical health of both the child and the adult. To show respect for the developing sense of beauty, to aid the growing independence, and to inspire the child to activity, we choose the best of everything for the environment.

It is important that the environment in the school reflect the time and culture of the children, as well as exposing them to the cultures of the world. The classroom should mirror the homes of each particular country or state: utensils, pottery, and fabrics, and so on will be unique to the area of the child. In schools the traditional Montessori sensorial and math materials will be the same colors and construction in any country, but the true creativity of the classroom comes in the selection of other materials. The teacher sometimes hems and embroiders the dusting cloths; the parents sometimes join in, and help find lovely trays and pottery that reflect the best that the culture has to offer, or introducing the arts of other cultures. Montessori classrooms should not look like they are bought in bulk from a factory. They should be inspired, individually created, and cherished by children and teacher alike.

The use of a floor mat or a table mat helps to delineate a work space, and also to mark the beginning and end of a project. This child in Bhutan is learning to roll up his mat and put it away when finished.

Age 3-6

Children at this age often prefer to work on the floor instead of at a table—on rugs or pieces of carpet that can be rolled up or put out of the way when not in use. This marks the workspace just as would a table. In the classroom and in the home toys, books, and materials are attractively arranged on trays and in baskets, on natural wood or white shelves according to subject—language, math, geography, history, science, music, and art. Each object has a special, permanent place so that children know where to find it and where to put it away for the next person when finished. Tables and chairs or stools that support proper posture are important at every age.

There are two important things to keep in mind in organizing a child's environment in the home.

First, have a place in each room for the few, carefully chosen child's belongings: By the front door a stool to sit on and a place to hang coats and keep shoes. In the living room a place for the child's books and toys — neatly, attractively organized. Think out the activities and the materials for all living spaces and arrange the environment to include the child's activities.

Secondly, don't put out too many toys and books at one time. Those being used by the child at the moment are sufficient. It is a good idea to rotate — taking out those books and toys that have not been chosen lately and removing them to storage for a time, sometimes with the help of the child. Children grow and change and they need help to keep their environment uncluttered and peaceful.

The environment affects everyone at every age. Habits of organizing the environment reduce stress and aid the development of an organized, efficient, and creative mind. The Chinese art of placement, or Feng Shui, teaches that clutter, even hidden under a bed or piled on the top of bookcases, is bad for a person. A child who joins in the arrangement of an environment, at school or at home, and learns to select a few lovely things instead of piles of unused toys, books, clothes, etc., will be aided in many ways with this help in creating good work habits, concentration, and a clear, uncluttered, and peaceful mind. The adult model is always the most important element in the environment. It is from observing what we do, not what we say, that the child will learn.

Age 6-12

At this age the child engages in many projects and needs a place, such as a clipboard, or a special cubby or shelf, to keep work. He needs the choice of spaces for silence or talking as each child has different needs for concentration and work. Whereas at age 3-6 the world was brought into the classroom, now the child begins to go out into the world, for field trips such as shopping at the grocery store for a cooking project, getting office supplies for the classroom, interviewing subjects for history projects, visiting museums, and so the teachers preparation includes research on the world outside the classroom.

Parenting and Teaching

*Children learn by watching us more than by any other way.
This youngster is by necessity carried on his father's back as he
works to polish the butter lamps in a temple in Bhutan.*

*I never teach my pupils; I only attempt to provide the
conditions in which they can learn.* — **Albert Einstein**

Montessori Materials may be divided into two main
categories. Didactic materials are those that were
developed by Dr. Montessori for use in schools. These
include basically the sensorial (pink tower, color tablets,
red rods, math beads, music bells, and many more)
materials. They are made by approved (and sometimes
unapproved) companies around the world and have
been tested for 100 years and found to work in the
classroom. They are not useful in the home because they

are of no value without a teacher trained on the relationship of their use to the needs of and development of the child.

The other category could be called adult-made materials. During a good teacher training the teacher is taught to analyze the culture of his or her class and find local materials, or make materials for the classroom. She learns to seek out the best local books, trays, cleaning supplies, etc. to link the child to that particular beauty and daily life in which they live. This creates a beautiful and unique environment instead of a mass-produced, boring look. Parents at home can do the same, creating a family-centered learning environment at home. With the information given in this book, *Child of the World*, hopefully the adult will be guided in finding culturally rich books, materials for the classroom and the home in the areas of music, art, history, geography, physics, and biology.

Many parents and teachers find themselves tempted to purchase more materials than are needed. This is sometimes called "the supermarket effect." This is not only wasteful, but it is damaging to the child's development. Authentic Montessori classrooms, where the only materials are those introduced during teacher training, prove to have children who are happy, focused, and with the longest periods of concentration—the best results overall. It is the same in the home. As long as the adults are following the interests of the child, and providing a balanced exposure to all of the areas we have discussed, usually less is better.

Through our children, we parents and teachers are the architects of the future of humanity. As we go about our daily lives in the presence of children we are constantly teaching by our own words, thoughts, and behavior. Education is sometimes narrowly defined as the teaching of math, language, sciences and the arts, but the most important subjects to be mastered are: how to be a compassionate friend, to express care through thoughtfulness and good manners, to identify a problem and work hard to solve it, to know how to become happy. More than facts, we can help our children develop a love of learning, an ability to make intelligent and responsible choices; to concentrate and focus, and to do one's best to complete a task to the satisfaction of oneself rather than to please someone else.

It was the greatest discovery of Dr. Montessori that after completing a prolonged period of deep concentration and contemplation, a child often expressed a great joy and a desire to help others. I would like to repeat the quote from the beginning of this book.

When the children had completed an absorbing bit of work, they appeared rested and deeply pleased. It almost seemed as if a road had opened up within their souls that led to all their latent powers, revealing the better part of themselves. They exhibited a great affability to everyone, put

*themselves out to help others, and seemed full of good
will.*

— Maria Montessori

Perhaps this is what people who daily make time for prayer or meditation feel, and why we think of them as happier, more peaceful, and in some ways better human beings than those of us who just rush from one task to the next.

Lessons on morality, books on morality, gold stars, these exterior inducements to happiness and goodness are never as successful as a good night's sleep or a long period of concentrated work or contemplation during which the mind can process the day's input, solve problems at a deep level, and come out happy. The most important advice on parenting and teaching we can offer is to constantly watch for periods of concentration and contemplation in our children and protect these moments from interruption.

Each of us was born with an inner guide, and all the tools to use whatever is found in the environment to create a self-fulfilled individual. Even if our own schooling may not have been based on a respect for this inner guide, we can provide it for our children. We can create a marvelous environment, learn to observe and interpret our child's behavior to discover his or her needs, and get out of the way.

One of the most important attitudes to nurture is to see each child as a new being each day, forgetting the past and seeing only the potential for greatness. This is also the best way to look at ourselves. It is a lot to ask of the adult to provide everything a child needs, and we believe that some time should be allotted, perhaps at the beginning of each day, to getting mentally prepared for the task by praying, meditating, taking a walk. Then one is better able to take a deep breath and face the day with a feeling of being new and in the present moment. If we can balance ourselves, our interactions with our children will be more enjoyable.

We are parents, grandparents, teachers, friends, or advocates of children, because we care about others. No matter how much we try to be perfect we must learn not to waste time wishing we "had only known earlier," but must learn to laugh, to pick up the pieces, and to begin again.

> *I had always understood that Madame Montessori dispensed with discipline and I wondered how she managed a room full of children.... On sending my little boy of three to spend his mornings in a Montessori school, I found that he quickly became a more disciplined human being.... The pedagogical discoveries involved have required genius but the teachers who are to apply them do not require genius. They require only the right sort of training, together with a degree of sympathy and patience, which is by no means unusual. The fundamental idea is simple: that the right discipline consists not in external compulsion, but in habits of mind, which lead spontaneously to desirable rather*

than undesirable activities. What is astonishing is
the great success in finding technical methods of
embodying this idea in education. For this, Madame
Montessori deserves the highest praise.
— **Bertrand Russell, philosopher**

The most important consideration in deciding to set up a Montessori class is the teacher. A non-Montessori-trained teacher can no more be expected to teach "Montessori" than a biologist could be expected to teach French. Using the Montessori approach to teach is extremely challenging, but equally exciting and rewarding. Montessori schools have proven successful all over the world, with all kinds of children (blind, gifted, learning disabled, wealthy, poor, etc.) and in many different environments (from refugee camps and slums to elegant schools in beautiful private homes).

Some Elements of Montessori Practice:

Multi-aged Grouping, based on Periods of Development: Children are grouped in three or six-year spans and have the same teacher all of the years.

The 3-Hour Work Period: At every age, a minimum of one 3-hour work period per day, uninterrupted by required attendance at *any* group activities, is necessary when using the Montessori method of education to produce the results for which the method is famous.

The Prepared Environment: The environment is logically arranged according to subject area. There are no textbooks, but instead approved didactic materials and a selection of culturally rich books and activities. Since the child learns to glean information from many sources, instead of being handed it by the teacher, it is the role of the teacher to prepare and continue to adapt the environment, to link the child to it through well-thought-out lessons, facilitating the child's exploration and creativity.

Teaching Method: children are always free to move around the room, and to continue to work on a piece of material with no time limit. Seldom will two or more children be studying the same thing at the same time. Children learn directly from the environment, and from other children — and from clear presentations of individual activities by the teacher. The child is scientifically observed, observations recorded and then studied by the teacher. The teacher is adept at teaching one child at a time, with occasional small groups and almost no lessons given to the whole class. She is facile in the basic lessons of math, language, the arts and sciences, and in guiding a child's research and exploration, capitalizing on a child's interests of the moment and excitement about a subject.

Large groups occur only when starting a new class, or in the beginning of the school year, and are phased out as the children gain independence. Children learn from what they are studying individually, from group projects that they initiate, and from the amazing variety of work that is going on around them during the day.

Class Size: The most successful 3-6 and 6-12 classes *if* the teacher is fully trained in the method — are of 30-35 children to one teacher, with one non-teaching assistant; this number reached gradually over time. This provides the most variety of personalities, learning styles, and work being done at one time. This class size is possible because the children learn from each other and stay with the same teacher for three (3-6) to six (6-12) years. Although laws sometimes prohibit this ratio laws have been changed in a few states to allow it.

Areas of Study Linked: All subjects are interwoven; history, art, music, math, astronomy, biology, geology, physics, and chemistry are not isolated from each other and a child studies them in any order he chooses, moving through all in a unique way for each child. At any one time in a day all subjects — math, language, science, history, geography, art, music, etc. — are being studied, at all levels.

Assessment: There are no grades, or other forms of reward or punishment, subtle or overt. Assessment is by portfolio and the teacher's observation and record keeping. The real test of whether or not the system is working lies in the accomplishment and behavior of the children, their happiness, maturity, kindness, love of learning, and their love of concentration and doing their best.

Requirements for age 3-6: There are no academic requirements for this age, but children are exposed to amazing amounts of knowledge and often learn to read, write and calculate beyond what is thought usual for a child of this age.

Requirements for ages 6-12: There are no curriculum requirements except those set by the state, or college entrance requirements, for specific grades and these take a minimum amount of time. Students design one or two-week contracts with the teacher to balance their work, and learn time management skills. The work of the 6-12 class includes subjects usually not introduced until high school.

Homework is not required, but sometimes children choose to continue to read a book, or continue to work on a project on their own or with friends outside school hours. This is difficult for parents to understand sometimes, but when we realize that, rather than the traditional 50-minute classes with a lot of wasted time, children are learning all day long, it makes sense. Many people applaud the fact that children in this system of education have time to participate in the family work, to relax, to spend time with their relatives and friends, instead of being required to devote time outside a full day at school to study.

Learning styles: All intelligences and styles of learning — musical, bodily kinesthetic, spatial, interpersonal, intrapersonal, intuitive, natural, and the traditional linguistic and logical-mathematical — are nurtured and respected.

Social/Character education: Opportunities for the strengthening of the personality is considered at least as important as academic education. Children are given the opportunity to take care of themselves, each other, and the environment — gardening, cooking, building, moving gracefully, speaking politely, doing social work in the community, etc.

The results: In looking at the results one must be sure they are judging a class run by a fully trained teacher. Using Montessori without this training will not have the same results. When the environment meets all of the needs of children they become, without any manipulation by the adult, physically healthy, mentally and psychologically fulfilled, extremely well educated, and brimming over with joy and kindness toward each other.

MARIA MONTESSORI

Montessori has spread around the world. This is a picture of the first group of Tibetan Montessori teachers in India with the late A.M. Joosten in 1970.

Maria Montessori was born in Italy in 1870 and became the first female medical doctor in this country. In her work at the University of Rome's psychiatric clinic, Dr. Montessori developed an interest in the treatment of children and for several years wrote and spoke on their behalf. At age twenty-eight, she became the director of a school for mentally disabled children. After two years under her guidance, these children, who formerly had been considered uneducable, took a school examination along with normal children and passed successfully. Educators called Dr. Montessori a miracle worker. What was her response? If mentally disabled children could be brought to the level of normal children, what does that say about the education of our normal children? For the rest of her life she conducted research, trained teachers, and continually discovered the secrets of the life of children. Her message was always to "follow the child."

Today, when traditional education is stretched to the limit in trying to prepare children for an unpredictable future, educators seek after Montessori education because of its emphasis on teaching children *how* to learn rather than *what* to learn, and its success in meeting the mental, physical, and emotional needs of children. But the struggle is always between maintaining the best of Montessori education and at the same time reaching more and more children. There have been many compromises and failures, but many successes.

Early in the movement Dr. Montessori observed the problems with moving too quickly, compromising too much, and so in 1929 created an organization to be consistent in standards of teacher training. This is the AMI or Association Montessori Internationale in Amsterdam. In many countries there are school and training centers that adhere to these standards, and works with other Montessori organizations throughout the world to help children. One of the main goals of the AMI organization today, according to the website (http://www.montessori-ami.org), is:

> *To function as a social movement that will strive to obtain recognition for the rights of the child throughout the world, irrespective of race, religion, political and social beliefs; co-operating with other bodies and organisations which further the development of education, human rights and peace.*

It is my hope the information in this book will help everyone who reads it to understand and appreciate what we all went through as children, and to provide the best that we can for the children of the world who exist now, and who are to follow. In closing I would like to quote Dr. Montessori's book, *The Absorbent Mind*, because no one puts my hopes for the future more eloquently.

> *In our first schools the children used to enter when three years old. No one could teach them because they were not receptive; yet they offered us amazing revelations of the greatness of the human soul. Ours was a house for children, rather than a real school. We had prepared a place for children where a diffused culture could be assimilated from the environment, without any need for direct instruction. The children who came were from the humblest social levels, and their parents were illiterate. Yet these children learned to read and write before they were five, and no one had given them any lessons. If visitors asked them, 'Who taught you to write?' they often answered with astonishment: 'Taught me? No one has taught me!' At that time it seemed miraculous that children of four and a half should be able to write, and that they should have learned without the feeling of having been taught.*
>
> *The press began to speak of 'culture acquired spontaneously.' Psychologists wondered if these children were somehow different from others, and we ourselves puzzled over it for a long time. Only after*

repeated experiments did we conclude with certainty that all children are endowed with this capacity to 'absorb' culture. If this be true, we then argued, if culture can be acquired without effort, let us provide the children with other elements of culture. And then we saw them 'absorb' far more than reading and writing: botany, zoology, mathematics, geography, and with the same ease, spontaneously and without getting tired.

And so we discovered that education is not something which the teacher does, but that it is a natural process which develops spontaneously in the human being. It is not acquired by listening to words, but in virtue of experiences in which the child acts on his environment. The teacher's task is not to talk, but to prepare and arrange a series of motives for cultural activity in a special environment made for the child.

If we follow these rules, the child, instead of being a burden, shows himself to us as the greatest and most consoling of nature's wonders! We find ourselves confronted by a being no longer to be thought of as helpless, like a receptive void waiting to be filled with our wisdom; but one whose dignity increases in the measure to which we see in him the builder of our own minds; one guided by his inward teacher, who labours indefatigably in joy and happiness, following a precise timetable, at the work of constructing that greatest marvel of the Universe, the human being.

We teachers can only help the work going on, as servants wait upon a master. We then become witnesses to the development of the human soul; the emergence of the New Man, who will no longer be the victim of events but thanks to his clarity of vision, will become able to direct and to mold the future of mankind.

ABOUT THE AUTHOR

On October 22, 1963, Susan Mayclin (Stephenson) sailed out of the New York Harbor on the maiden voyage of the University of the Seven Seas, today known as the Semester at Sea program. 275 students visited 22 ports in Europe, the Middle East, North Africa, and Asia. Overwhelmed by what she had seen in slums, orphanages, hospitals, and homes, Susan retuned home determined to find a way to help children have a better life. She came to Montessori through her first child when the three-year-old began to attend a Montessori school in San Francisco. Her daughter's developing independence and ability to concentrate and become happy under her own efforts, convinced Susan that being a Montessori teacher might just hold the key to her desire.

Susan has degrees in philosophy, comparative religions, and education, and in 1971, in London, England she was awarded the AMI (Association Montessori Internationale) diploma for teaching children from 2.5-6 years of age. Since then she has earned the 0-3 and 6-12 diplomas, worked with children from birth through age 18 and with adults. She is a wife, mother, grandmother, and artist, and has continued to learn and share her insights gained in more than 70 countries. Her website is www.susanart.net

(Photo: Susan in the Middle East in 2010)

ACCLAIM FOR CHILD OF THE WORLD

Following the child in a Montessori way from the beginning is like finding a pearl in your pocket. The Montessori philosophy is so beautiful and precious that puts you on a wonderful journey of mindful parenting. We truly treasure the Child of the World *as our point of reference in all ways.*

— Daniele and Aika W. Mariani Montessori parents, Italy

Teachers at Shree Mangal Dvip School were fortunate to attend seminars on education and child development given by Susan Stephenson in Kathmandu, Nepal. Her insightful presentation inspired its administration to begin reforming its program to include Montessori ideals and practices. An invaluable resource for all things Montessori, Susan has shared her thoughtful delineation of the Montessori approach and its practices in one indispensable volume, Child of the World, *a veritable source of wisdom and guidance for parents, teachers, and administrators.*

— Riza Weinstein, Canadian supporter of the SMD school in Nepal

It would be great if many parents, relatives, and teachers dedicated their time to reading this great book about children. Everybody would benefit from this precious guide and consequently would live in a more peaceful, happy, and loveable environment.

— Eva Prado, mother and teacher, Brazil

The engineer in me was drawn to the fact that Dr. Maria Montessori's discoveries came through years of scientific observation. If all children, independent of country, ethnicity, or economic background, get their first

160

tooth around 6 months and start to walk around their first birthday, doesn't it make sense that there would be "universal truths" for children's cognitive development, too? As a parent, my job is to prepare an environment that will allow my child to develop into the best version of himself.

— Jean Layton Rosas, Intel software engineer, USA

The explanation of Montessori education in Child of the World *helps us understand that in seeking the best of modern academic education, we must not lose what we had in the past, and still have in some places. In rural areas and villages of Palestine, children stay close to their parents, watching and imitating their work. Usually each villager has a plot of land around the house, which is mostly the responsibility of the women, for growing a kitchen garden and keeping a few chickens for eggs and for meat. Children get involved, feeding the chickens, giving them water, and collecting eggs. They are usually taught some of the household functions and mothers and elder women often teach young girls knitting and/or traditional embroidery. The father might make boys and girls rudimentary agricultural tools or buy them tiny brooms that they can use to help. Thank you for reminding us to hold on to our traditions.*

— Hani Abudayyeh, a father, Palestine

This is an excellent educational resource. I have used it extensively in homeschooling my own child (and the children of others). Child of the World *is an excellent tool in ensuring a child a well-rounded education.*

— Carol Ann McKinley, Montessori teacher, New Zealand

Susan Stephenson's explanation of Montessori practice and philosophy is both readable and inspiring. Her writing is a useful response to questions or criticism often heard regarding Montessori education, that it is either too rigid or not rigid enough. In simple terms, she goes to the heart of what a successful Montessori education involves: the child taking the lead in her own education. Ms. Stephenson has dedicated her life to the furtherance of Montessori education around the world. This book demonstrates how the Montessori method transcends different cultures to bring the focus to the child.

—Miriam Geraghty, civil rights lawyer and mother, USA

I agree with every word, and in my dream Israel and the whole region will learn peace and living together from early childhood on. All the fears that come from the unknown will just disappear. Montessori is a truth that can and should be shared by all children regardless of their background. Peace might then be a real possibility even in our region.

— Ariella Beer, Israel

On a continent where children are yet to be seen fully for the gifts they are, Child of the World *offers a guiding light. Thank you for the inspiration you continue to provide.*

—Samantha Streak, South Africa

Young parents and educators desiring information on early childhood educational options will be thrilled to discover Child of the World. *The philosophy promoted by Maria Montessori since the early 1900's has survived and prospered because it was insightful and nurturing. Explaining*

Maria's constructivist approach in a delightful, easy to understand format, Susan makes us wish we could relive our childhood as a Montessori student. As we read, we feel the joy that little ones must feel in Montessori schools, where students are gently guided to learn in an environment of discovery, respect, and independence, where the very essence and spirit of children is cherished.

—Jan West, Peace Corps Volunteer, Afghanistan, Faculty, Humboldt State University, California

Child of the World *offers very good advice to support the Montessori lessons of practical life activities, sensorial experiences, language, math and geometry, art and music social studies, and the physical and life sciences, from age 3-12. It has been referred to as "a Montessori course in one volume." Susan Stephenson has been teaching in the Montessori field since 1970, has read all of Dr. Montessori's books, and has pulled out the quotes that are most helpful to parents and teachers. This book offers kind guidance along a sure path for development the skills and attributes that will assist a child in preparing for life. It is welcomed into Montessori training centers, schools, and homes worldwide as a clear and concise guide to basic Montessori principles.*

—Cathryn Kasper, AMI/USA Montessori school consultant

This book is an essential resource for everyone who works with children. We refer to these teachings again and again in our parent education program.

—Julia Volkman, Montessori Mentor, Zanetti Public Montessori School, Massachusetts, USA

I have known Susan for almost 30 years. I have found the information to be the highest quality. In Montessori we say that we respect the child. Respect is more than a high regard; it is doing something for the child's well being. Susan respects children in this very down to earth regard. She is doing something great!

— Rita Schaefer Zener, PhD, Director of AMI Montessori Training in several countries

One of the greatest gifts I can give my child is a clear and ordered mind. The Montessori approach to education, as explained in Child of the World, *guards the organization of that sacred space where learning happens.*

— Amy Miller Bazemore, International Baccalaureate (IB) teacher and musician, California, USA

Child of the World has always been part of our parent education programme: practical advice, reliable information and a source of fantastic ideas for parents, on how to prepare the home environment and what are appropriate toys/materials for the child at each stage of his development. It is truly full of wisdom.

— Heidi Philippart, Montessori teacher and school owner, Amsterdam

Made in the USA
Lexington, KY
27 August 2013